The *Writing Teacher's* BOOK OF LISTS

WITH READY-TO-USE ACTIVITIES AND WORKSHEETS

Gary Robert Muschla

PRENTICE HALL
Englewood Cliffs, New Jersey 07632

Prentice-Hall International (UK) Limited, *London*
Prentice-Hall of Australia Pty. Limited, *Sydney*
Prentice-Hall Canada, Inc., *Toronto*
Prentice-Hall Hispanoamericana, S.A., *Mexico*
Prentice-Hall of India Private Limited, *New Delhi*
Prentice-Hall of Japan, Inc., *Tokyo*
Simon & Schuster Asia Pte. Ltd., *Singapore*
Editora Prentice-Hall do Brasil, Ltda., *Rio de Janeiro*

© 1991 *by*

PRENTICE HALL
Englewood Cliffs, NJ

Thirty-seven of the illustrations within are reproductions from the fine
Dover Press Pictorial Archives Series. The reproductions are used with
the permission of Dover Publications, Inc.

10 9 8 7 6 5 4 3 2 1

Library of Congress Cataloging-in-Publication Data

Muschla, Gary Robert.
    The writing teacher's book of lists / Gary Robert Muschla.
       p.   cm.
    ISBN 0-13-971169-4
    1. English language—Writing—Study and teaching—Handbooks,
manuals, etc.   2. Teaching—Aids and devices—Handbooks, manuals,
etc.   3. Activity programs in education—Handbooks, manuals, etc.
I. Title
LB1576.M88   1991
808'.042'07—dc20   90-28580
                                                              CIP

ISBN 0-13-971169-4

PRENTICE HALL
BUSINESS & PROFESSIONAL DIVISION
A division of Simon & Schuster
Englewood Cliffs, New Jersey 07632

Printed in the United States of America

This book is for Judy and Erin, both of whom seem to gladly accept a writer in their lives.

About the Author

Gary Robert Muschla received his B.A. and M.A.T. from Trenton State College in New Jersey. For the past fifteen years, he has taught at Appleby School in the Spotswood, New Jersey School District, where he has developed a practical approach to the teaching of writing, conducted writing workshops for teachers and students, and edited magazines of students' writing.

In addition to his teaching experience, Mr. Muschla has been a successful freelance writer, editor, and ghostwriter. He is the author of the *Writing Resource Activities Kit: Ready-to-Use Worksheets and Enrichment Lessons for Grades 4–9* (The Center for Applied Research in Education, 1989).

Acknowledgments

I'd like to thank John C. Orlick, my principal, for his continued support. I'd also like to thank my colleague Joan Intravartolo for her encouragement, advice, and suggestions; and Ann Piro, whose library skills and willingness to help are most appreciated.

Special thanks are a must to my typist, Donna Cooper. Despite my reliance on word processors, she provided the final typing, making sure that all my last-minute insertions fit into the whole.

And most special thanks to my wife Judy, who assumed the task of obtaining and arranging the illustrations that liven these pages.

Finally, I'd like to thank my editor, Sandra Hutchison, whose insights and suggestions invariably enhanced this work.

Thanks also to Zsuzsa Neff, my production editor, who accepted the challenge and provided a fine design.

ABOUT THIS BOOK

Good writing is a skill. It can be learned and improved. While not all students have the ability to become professional writers, most can acquire effective writing skills that they can use throughout their lives.

It is your task to present activities and experiences that help students learn to write with clarity, confidence, and enjoyment. As many teachers have found, this can be a most difficult charge, for writing is a complex process.

The Writing Teacher's Book of Lists, therefore, has three important goals:

1. To be a resource that helps you teach writing more effectively.
2. To provide students with information and ideas that can help them improve their writing skills.
3. To provide meaningful activities that will help students develop an understanding of the writing process.

Writing is a basic skill that is closely linked to thinking and speaking. To write clearly, a person must first gather, sort, and analyze information. The information must then be organized so that it can be presented in a way that best expresses the ideas and purpose of the writer. These are fundamental skills crucial to success in various disciplines.

The skills necessary for effective writing can be learned and improved. All stories and articles have basic parts that can be constructed and managed by the writer. Students can do this, but they must be shown how. Without question, given the proper direction and experiences, students can acquire the skills that will enable them to express themselves clearly and efficiently. I'd like to extend to you my best wishes as you embark on this vital undertaking.

Gary Robert Muschla

HOW TO USE THIS BOOK

The Writing Teacher's Book of Lists is divided into six sections containing a total of seventy-four lists. Some of the lists are accompanied by sublists or background information that expands the material of the original list.

The lists of the first five sections include teaching suggestions and ready-to-use writing activities. The teaching suggestions provide valuable information, methods, and techniques for teaching writing, while the activities enable your students to improve their writing skills as they apply the knowledge gained from the lists. The lists may be used to help generate ideas as well as to serve as vocabulary files. Because the topics of the writing activities focus on subjects that are familiar to students, anxiety levels are kept low and the writing is made easier. Reproducible worksheets provide variety and broaden the scope of the activities.

Section VI contains reference lists for both you and your students. These lists include helpful and interesting information that you can distribute as necessary. For example, if you wish to share with your class titles of books for students about writers and writing, hand out List 50. If you are interested in books about teaching writing, check List 51, which is provided for teachers. List 73 contains a writer's glossary, which can aid in discussing writing as a profession, while List 74 contains a breakdown of the writing process.

A major strength of *The Writing Teacher's Book of Lists* is its flexibility and ease of utilization. The lists are designed to be used with students of various grades and abilities. Because each list stands alone, you are able to employ the materials of the book as necessary to accommodate the needs of your students. Moreover, the lists are cross-referenced so that you can refer to additional material should you wish to expand concepts or provide more information through a related topic. The book can be used either as the foundation of your writing program, or it can supplement your language curriculum.

Most people will find that working through the book in order will provide their students with an effective writing experience. Section I, "Lists and Activities for Special Words and Word Groups," for instance, provides students with basic knowledge about notable words and offers activities that will foster in them an understanding of the richness of the English language. The skills they learn in this section will help them to write better on later assignments.

While many teachers will find it best to use the book sequentially, others will find that matching the lists and activities to their language programs will be most effective. If your class is advanced, you might begin with Section V, " 'Check' Lists and Activities for Writers." This section is designed to help the more competent writer refine his or her ability by focusing on such topics as prewriting, organization, revision, and proofreading. You can then assign other activities to fit your plans. Since each list and its activities form a self-contained lesson, you can use what you need when you need it.

The lists, activities, and reproducible worksheets on the following pages will undoubtedly provide your students with a variety of writing experiences. *The Writing Teacher's Book of Lists* will enhance your writing program and make your teaching of writing easier and more effective.

CONTENTS

About This Book   vi

How to Use This Book   vii

Skills Index   xvii

**Section I   LISTS AND ACTIVITIES FOR SPECIAL WORDS
AND WORD GROUPS**   1

1   **SYNONYMS**   3
    Teaching Suggestions
    Activity 1—My Favorite Thing to Do
    Activity 2—Creating Synonym Word Finds
    List 1—Synonyms

2   **ANTONYMS**   8
    Teaching Suggestions
    Activity 1—A Matter of Character
    Activity 2—Creating Antonym Word Finds
    List 2—Antonyms

3   **HOMOGRAPHS**   12
    Teaching Suggestions
    Activity 1—Worksheet 3–1, "The Concert"
    List 3—Homographs

4   **HOMOPHONES**   16
    Teaching Suggestions
    Activity—Worksheet 4–1, "Jennifer's Party"
    List 4—Homophones

5   **HARD-TO-SPELL WORDS (INTERMEDIATE)**   22
    Teaching Suggestions
    Activity 1—A Time When I Was Really Angry
    Activity 2—Maintaining Personal Spelling Lists
    List 5—Hard to Spell Words (Intermediate)

  6 **HARD-TO-SPELL WORDS (ADVANCED)**   **26**
     Teaching Suggestions
     Activity 1—My Dream Date
     Activity 2—Spelling Bee with a Twist
     List 6—Hard-to-Spell Words (Advanced)

  7 **EASILY CONFUSED WORDS**   **31**
     Teaching Suggestions
     Activity—Worksheet 7–1, "Spaceman in the Backyard"
     List 7—Easily Confused Words

  8 **SOUND WORDS**   **38**
     Teaching Suggestions
     Activity 1—Sound Poems
     Activity 2—A Listening Adventure
     List 8—Sound Words

  9 **COMPOUND WORDS**   **41**
     Teaching Suggestions
     Activity 1—Worksheet 9–1, "Cookies for the Class Trip"
     Activity 2—How Many Can You Find?
     List 9—Compound Words

 10 **SENSORY WORDS**   **46**
     Teaching Suggestions
     Activity 1—Now Feelings
     Activity 2—In the Eye of the Beholder
     Activity 3—It's So Good . . .
     List 10—Sensory Words

 11 **TIME WORDS**   **50**
     Teaching Suggestions
     Activity 1—A Diary of Today
     Activity 2—An Autobiographical Sketch
     List 11—Time Words

     Section II LISTS AND ACTIVITIES FOR NONFICTION WRITING   **53**

 12 **ADVERTISING WORDS**   **55**
     Teaching Suggestions
     Activity 1—Worksheet 12–1, "Being an Ad Writer"
     Activity 2—Write a Classified Ad
     List 12—Advertising Words

 13 **BUSINESS WORDS**   **59**
     Teaching Suggestions
     Activity 1—Worksheet 13–1, "Starting Your Own Business"

Activity 2—A Profile of Success
List 13—Business Words

14 CONSUMER WORDS   **62**
Teaching Suggestions
Activity 1—Worksheet 14–1, "Being a Smart Consumer"
Activity 2—A Letter to the Company
List 14—Consumer Words
Background Sheet 14, Sample Business-Letter Forms

15 CRAFT WORDS   **67**
Teaching Suggestions
Activity 1—Worksheet 15–1, "I Made It"
Activity 2—The How and Why of Doing a Craft
List 15—Craft Words

16 ECOLOGY WORDS   **70**
Teaching Suggestions
Activity 1—Worksheet 16–1, "A Speech About the Environment"
Activity 2—Changing Places
List 16—Ecology Words

17 EDUCATION WORDS   **74**
Teaching Suggestions
Activity 1—Worksheet 17–1, "What's Right and Wrong with My School"
Activity 2—If I Were a Teacher
List 17—Education Words

18 FOOD WORDS   **78**
Teaching Suggestions
Activity 1—Worksheet 18–1, "It's Time to Feast"
Activity 2—Make a Meal Plan
List 18—Food Words

19 WORDS OF GOVERNMENT AND POLITICS   **83**
Teaching Suggestions
Activity 1—Worksheet 19–1, "Personal Policies"
Activity 2—A Student Bill of Rights
List 19—Words of Government and Politics

20 HEALTH WORDS   **87**
Teaching Suggestions
Activity 1—Worksheet 20–1, "A Subject of Health"
Activity 2—How to Get Along with People
List 20—Health Words

21 HOBBY WORDS   **91**
Teaching Suggestions
Activity 1—Worksheet 21–1, "My Hobby"

Activity 2—After-School Activities
List 21—Hobby Words

22 WORDS OF NEWSPAPERS AND MAGAZINES   95
Teaching Suggestions
Activity 1—Worksheet 22–1, "Get the Scoop!"
Activity 2—Write an Editorial
List 22—Words of Newspapers and Magazines
Background Sheet 22, Tips for Effective Interviews

23 SPORTS WORDS   100
Teaching Suggestions
Activity 1—Worksheet 23–1, "The Rules and Strategies of the Game"
Activity 2—Be a Sportswriter
List 23—Sports Words

24 TRAVEL WORDS   104
Teaching Suggestions
Activity 1—Worksheet 24–1, "Traveling Around"
Activity 2—An Imaginary Trip
List 24—Travel Words

Section III   LISTS AND ACTIVITIES FOR FICTION WRITING   107

25 WORDS OF ADVENTURE AND ROMANCE   109
Teaching Suggestions
Activity 1—Worksheet 25–1, "The Continuing Adventures of . . ."
Activity 2—The Complete Character
List 25—Words of Adventure and Romance

26 WORDS OF FOLKLORE   113
Teaching Suggestions
Activity 1—Worksheet 26–1, "Inventing a Folk Tale"
Activity 2—A Local Legend
List 26—Words of Folklore

27 WORDS OF MYTHOLOGY   118
Teaching Suggestions
Activity 1—Worksheet 27–1, "Modern Myths"
Activity 2—Nature Myths
List 27—Words of Mythology

28 WORDS OF PLAYS   122
Teaching Suggestions
Activity—Play Writing
List 28—Words of Plays
Background Sheet 28, A Simple Structure for a Play

29 WORDS OF SCIENCE FICTION AND FANTASY   **125**
Teaching Suggestions
Activity 1—Worksheet 29–1, "A Story About the Fantastic"
Activity 2—A Review of Science Fiction or Fantasy
List 29—Words of Science Fiction and Fantasy

30 SPY, DETECTIVE, AND MYSTERY WORDS   **130**
Teaching Suggestions
Activity 1—Worksheet 30–1, "Making a Hero"
Activity 2—A Mysterious Occurrence
List 30—Spy, Detective, and Mystery Words

31 WESTERN WORDS   **134**
Teaching Suggestions
Activity 1—Worksheet 31–1, "Writing a Western"
Activity 2—Going Backward in Time
List 31—Western Words

Section IV   LISTS AND ACTIVITIES FOR WRITING STYLE   **137**

32 PHRASES OF ALLITERATION   **139**
Teaching Suggestions
Activity 1—Worksheet 32–1, "My Kind of Music"
Activity 2—A Big Storm
List 32—Phrases of Alliteration

33 ANALOGIES   **142**
Teaching Suggestions
Activity 1—Worksheet 33–1, "Check the Relationship"
Activity 2—Creating Analogies
List 33—Analogies

34 CLICHÉS   **146**
Teaching Suggestions
Activity 1—Worksheet 34–1, "The Major Mix-Up"
Activity 2—Mistakes Parents Make
List 34—Clichés

35 FIGURES OF SPEECH   **152**
Teaching Suggestions
Activity 1—Worksheet 35–1, "An Enjoyable Day"
Activity 2—A Nightmare Poem
List 35—Figures of Speech

36 JARGON   **156**
Teaching Suggestions
Activity 1—Worksheet 36–1, "Planning Your Future"

Activity 2—Fun with Jargon
List 36—Jargon

37   OVERBLOWN (REDUNDANT) PHRASES   **161**
Teaching Suggestions
Activity 1—Worksheet 37–1, "Lost on Mars"
Activity 2—Worksheet 37–2, "The Big Test"
Activity 3—Images
List 37—Overblown (Redundant) Phrases

38   SEQUENTIAL WORDS AND PHRASES   **167**
Teaching Suggestions
Activity 1—Worksheet 38–1, "A Great Responsibility"
Activity 2—Follow My Instructions
List 38—Sequential Words and Phrases

39   TRANSITIONAL WORDS AND PHRASES   **170**
Teaching Suggestions
Activity 1—Worksheet 39–1, "Highlights"
Activity 2—Why Students Succeed (or Fail)
List 39—Transitional Words and Phrases

Section V   "CHECK" LISTS AND ACTIVITIES FOR WRITERS   **175**

40   PREWRITING CHECKLIST   **177**
Teaching Suggestions
Activity 1—Worksheet 40–1, "It's Your Pick"
Activity 2—Changes
List 40—Prewriting Checklist
Background Sheet 40, Simple Outline Format

41   TARGET AUDIENCE CHECKLIST   **183**
Teaching Suggestions
Activity 1—Worksheet 41–1, "A Personal Message"
Activity 2—Persuading Your Peers
List 41—Target Audience Checklist

42   CHECKLIST FOR ORGANIZING NONFICTION   **187**
Teaching Suggestions
Activity 1—Worksheet 42–1, "The Person Who Made a Difference in My
  Life"
Activity 2—Group Reviewing
List 42—Checklist for Organizing Nonfiction Writing

43   CHECKLIST FOR REVISION   **191**
Teaching Suggestions
Activity 1—Worksheet 43–1, "It's Tough Being Young"

Activity 2—Revise the Essay
List 43—Checklist for Revision
Worksheet 43–2, Revision Rating Sheet

44 CHECKLIST FOR REVISING FICTION 196
Teaching Suggestions
Activity 1—Worksheet 44–1, "The Guest"
Activity 2—Self-Editing
List 44—Checklist for Revising Fiction

45 PROOFREADING CHECKLIST 200
Teaching Suggestions
Activity 1—Worksheet 45–1, "The New Kid in Town"
Activity 2—Proofreading Practice
List 45—Proofreading Checklist

Section VI LISTS FOR REFERENCE 205

List 46 PROMOTING THE "WRITE" ATMOSPHERE 207

List 47 ANNOTATED LIST OF LIBRARY REFERENCES 209

List 48 BIBLIOGRAPHY FORMAT 212

List 49 FOOTNOTE/ENDNOTE FORMAT 213

List 50 BOOKS FOR STUDENTS ABOUT WRITERS AND WRITING 214

List 51 BOOKS AND RESOURCES ABOUT TEACHING WRITING 216

List 52 COMMON FOREIGN WORDS AND PHRASES 218

List 53 MAJOR GENRES OR FICTION 220

List 54 GRADING THE WRITING OF YOUR STUDENTS 221

List 55 QUESTIONS TO HELP FOCUS WRITING TOPICS 224

List 56 COMMON INITIALIZATIONS 226

List 57 JOBS IN WHICH WRITING IS AN IMPORTANT SKILL 227

List 58 MARKETS FOR THE WRITING OF STUDENTS 229

List 59 PLAGARISM AND HOW TO AVOID IT 232

List 60 PLAY FORMAT 233

List 61   POETRY FORMATS (INTERMEDIATE GRADES)   235

List 62   POETRY FORMATS (ADVANCED GRADES)   237

List 63   EDITOR'S PROOFREADING MARKS   239

List 64   QUOTES ABOUT WRITING   240

List 65   SCREENPLAY FORMAT   242

List 66   TOPICS FOR LITERATURE RESEARCH PAPERS   246

List 67   STEPS FOR DOING A RESEARCH PAPER   250

List 68   TYPES OF WRITING   251

List 69   WRITING ACTIVITIES FOR OTHER SUBJECTS   252

List 70   WAYS TO PUBLISH THE WORK OF YOUR STUDENTS   255

List 71   TIPS FOR ANSWERING ESSAY TESTS   256

List 72   GUIDELINES FOR WRITER'S CONFERENCES   257

List 73   WRITER'S GLOSSARY   259

List 74   THE WRITING PROCESS   263

SKILLS INDEX

For your convenience, the following skills are listed alphabetically.

Alliteration

    My Kind of Music (List 32, Worksheet 32–1)
    A Big Storm (List 32)

Analogies

    Check the Relationship (List 33, Worksheet 33–1)
    Creating Analogies (List 33)

Antonyms

    Creating Antonym Word Finds (List 2)

Characterization

    A Matter of Character (List 2)
    The Complete Character (List 25)
    Making a Hero (List 30, Worksheet 30–1)

Clichés

    The Major Mix-Up (List 34, Worksheet 34–1)
    Mistakes Parents Make (List 34)

Compound Words

    Cookies for the Class Trip (List 9, Worksheet 9–1)
    How Many Can You Find? (List 9)

Descriptive Writing

A Listening Adventure (List 8)
Now Feelings (List 10)
In the Eye of the Beholder (List 10)
It's So Good . . . (List 10)
Being a Smart Consumer (List 14, Worksheet 14–1)
I Made It (List 15, Worksheet 15–1)
The How and Why of Doing a Craft (List 15)
Images (List 37)
A Great Responsibility (List 38, Worksheet 38–1)
Follow My Instructions (List 38)
Why Students Succeed (or Fail) (List 39)

Editing

Self-Editing (List 44)

Editorial Writing

Write an Editorial (List 22)
A Personal Message (List 41, Worksheet 41–1)
Persuading Your Peers (List 41)

Fiction Writing

Changing Places (List 16)
An Imaginary Trip (List 24)
The Continuing Adventures of . . . (List 25, Worksheet 25–1)
Inventing a Folk Tale (List 26, Worksheet 26–1)
A Local Legend (List 26)
Modern Myths (List 27, Worksheet 27–1)
Nature Myths (List 27)
A Story About the Fantastic (List 29, Worksheet 29–1)
Writing a Western (List 31, Worksheet 31–1)
Going Backward in Time (List 31)

Figures of Speech

An Enjoyable Day (List 35, Worksheet 35–1)
A Nightmare Poem (List 35)

Homographs

The Concert (List 3, Worksheet 3–1)

Homophones

Jennifer's Party (List 4, Worksheet 4–1)

Letter Writing

A Letter to the Company (List 14)

Newspaper Article Writing

Get the Scoop (List 22, Worksheet 22–1)
Be a Sportswriter (List 23)

Nonfiction Writing

Being an Ad Writer (List 12, Worksheet 12–1)
Write a Classified Ad (List 12)
Starting Your Own Business (List 13, Worksheet 13–1)
A Profile of Success (List 13)
What's Right and Wrong with My School (List 17, Worksheet 17–1)
If I Were a Teacher (List 17)
It's Time to Feast (List 18, Worksheet 18–1)
Make a Meal Plan (List 18)
Personal Policies (List 19, Worksheet 19–1)
A Student Bill of Rights (List 19)
A Subject of Health (List 20, Worksheet 20–1)
How to Get Along with People (List 20)
My Hobby (List 21, Worksheet 21–1)
After-School Activities (List 21)
The Rules and Strategies of the Game (List 23, Worksheet 23–1)
Traveling Around (List 24, Worksheet 24–1)

Personal Accounts

A Diary of Today (List 11)
An Autobiographical Sketch (List 11)
A Mysterious Occurrence (List 30)
It's Your Pick (List 40, Worksheet 40–1)
Changes (List 40)
The Person Who Made a Difference in My Life (List 42, Worksheet 42–1)

Plays

Play Writing (List 28)
Complete a Play (List 60)

Poetry

Sound Poems (List 8)
A Nightmare Poem (List 35)

Proofreading

The New Kid in Town (List 45, Worksheet 45–1)
Proofreading Practice (List 45)

Reviews

A Review of Science Fiction or Fantasy (List 29)

Revision

Planning Your Future (List 36, Worksheet 36–1)
Fun with Jargon (List 36)
Lost on Mars (List 37, Worksheet 37–1)
The Big Test (List 37, Worksheet 37–2)
It's Tough Being Young (List 43, Worksheet 43–1)
Revise the Essay (List 43)
The Guest (List 44, Worksheet 44–1)

Screenplays

Complete a Screenplay (List 65)

Speech Writing

A Speech About the Environment (List 16, Worksheet 16–1)

Spelling

A Time When I Was Really Angry (List 5)
Maintaining Personal Spelling Lists (List 5)
My Dream Date (List 6)
Spelling Bee with a Twist (List 6)

Synonyms

My Favorite Thing to Do (List 1)
Creating Synonym Word Finds (List 1)

Transitions

Highlights (List 39, Worksheet 39–1)
Why Students Succeed (or Fail) (List 39)

Word Usage

Spaceman in the Backyard (List 7, Worksheet 7–1)

Lists and Activities for Special Words and Word Groups

1

SYNONYMS

Teaching Suggestions

Synonyms are words that have similar meanings. An understanding of synonyms expands the vocabulary of students and can help them find precise words that clearly communicate their ideas. In discussing synonyms with your students, be sure to emphasize that dictionaries and thesauruses are good sources in which to find words that have similar meanings.

ACTIVITY 1 — MY FAVORITE THING TO DO

Objective:

Students are to select one of their favorite pastimes and write a descriptive paragraph about it.

Procedure:

Distribute copies of List 1 and briefly review synonyms with your students. Next, ask them to think of a favorite pastime. What do they like to do most? You might ask for volunteers to share their favorite activities and write these on the board. This will help generate ideas as well as enthusiasm.

For the assignment, students are to write ten words that describe their pastime. They are then to write at least two synonyms for each word in an attempt to find the very best words that describe their pastime. After they have done this, they are to write a paragraph describing their favorite pastime.

ACTIVITY 2 — CREATING SYNONYM WORD FINDS

Objective:

Students are to create synonym word finds.

Procedure:

Hand out copies of List 1 and discuss synonyms with your students. For the assignment, tell them that they will be making word finds. These are not just simple word finds, however; there is a catch—they must have at least *twelve* words.

While students should be free to make their puzzles in any shape they wish, tell them that simple squares or rectangles are easiest to work with. You may pass out graph paper to facilitate the making of the puzzles. The words of the puzzle may run right to left, left to right, upward, downward, or diagonally.

At the bottom of the puzzle, students are to include a word bank. However, the words in the word bank will not be the words found in the puzzles. Instead, words in the puzzle will be synonyms of the words in the word bank. To find the words in the puzzles, one must find the synonyms of the words in the word bank. Students may use the synonyms of List 1, or they may use their own words.

If you wish, you may make copies of the completed word finds and have a Synonym Word Find Party, allowing students to work out each other's puzzles. You may also decide to collect the puzzles and produce a class word find book, and then distribute copies to other classes.

See List 2, Antonyms.

List 1. Synonyms

Synonyms are words that are similar in meaning. Sometimes they are identical in meaning; sometimes they mean nearly the same thing. Dictionaries and thesauruses are good sources in which to find synonyms. Knowledge of synonyms enables a writer to find the word that best communicates his or her ideas. Following are some common synonyms.

abandon — desert	bright — brilliant
about — nearly	brook — creek
act — do	buddy — friend
add — sum	build — construct
after — following	call — summon
ambition — goal	calm — placid
answer — reply	capture — seize
approve — accept	carry — lug
ask — question	change — alter
attack — assault	children — youngsters
authoritative — commanding	close — shut
automaton — robot	clumsy — awkward
automobile — car	comfort — ease
back — rear	conscientious — responsible
baffle — puzzle	cramped — confined
barren — infertile	deal — bargain
before — prior to	dull — dim
betray — reveal	dumb — stupid
bewilder — confuse	eat — consume
bitter — stinging	elaborate — complex
bored — indifferent	elastic — flexible
boy — lad	end — finish
brave — valiant	enough — sufficient

every — all
fight — battle
food — nourishment
form — shape
fury — rage
girl — maiden
give — grant
goal — aim
good — suitable
great — grand
grow — mature
hard — rigid
have — possess
help — assist
high — lofty
idea — concept
incline — slant
incredible — unbelievable
join — unite
just — fair
kind — gentle
large — big
learn — understand
like — enjoy
little — small
long — lengthy
lovely — beautiful
man — male
mild — gentle
mistake — error
nation — country

naughty — bad
nautical — marine
near — close by
neat — orderly
new — recent
nimble — agile
now — immediately
ocean — sea
often — frequently
old — ancient
one — single
pain — ache
part — portion
picture — image
place — spot
plain — simple
play — frolic
power — strength
push — shove
put — set
quake — tremble
quick — rapid
reason — infer
relate — tell
right — correct
roar — bellow
say — state
seem — appear
shortened — abbreviated
show — display
start — begin

stop — cease

strong — sturdy

study — examine

suggest — advise

summit — peak

sure — certain

surprise — astound

tasty — delicious

teach — instruct

thin — slender

think — consider

time — period

tired — weary

tough — hardy

tricky — clever

uncommon — unusual

under — below

universe — cosmos

unlike — different

unwise — foolish

use — utilize

vacant — empty

vague — unclear

vain — conceited

valley — glen

vast — huge

verge — edge

vital — essential

vow — swear

want — desire

while — during

word — term

work — labor

world — globe

worry — anxiety

wrestle — grapple

write — record

yank — pull

zenith — summit

zero — nothing

2

ANTONYMS

Teaching Suggestions

Antonyms are words that are opposite in meaning. A basic understanding of antonyms not only broadens vocabulary, but is also helpful in making descriptions of and drawing comparisons between different things. Sometimes a student can find the exact word he or she needs to describe an idea by thinking of its opposite first.

In teaching antonyms, point out to your students that dictionaries and thesauruses are sources they can consult when they need information about antonyms.

ACTIVITY 1 — A MATTER OF CHARACTER

Objective:

Students are to select a hero or villain and write a descriptive paragraph about this person's opposite.

Procedure:

Distribute List 2 and discuss antonyms with your students. Explain that writers rely heavily on opposites. Almost every story is built around the conflict between opposites—the hero and the villain.

Next, ask your students to name some heroes and villains. They may name real people, historical figures, or characters from fiction. Discuss some of the traits of heroes and villains. You might list some of these on the board. Explain that writers use traits to create characters.

Now instruct your students to select a hero or a villain and write at least ten words that describe this character. After listing these ten words, have them write an antonym for each word. Using these antonyms, they are then to write a descriptive paragraph. Point out that they will be changing their heroes to villains and their villains to heroes. Through the use of antonyms, they have created opposite characters.

Extension:

You can easily expand this activity. After your students have written their descriptions, instruct them to write a story about the new character they have created.

ACTIVITY 2 — CREATING ANTONYM WORD FINDS

Objective:

Students are to create antonym word finds.

Procedure:

Hand out copies of List 2 and discuss antonyms with your students. Tell them that they will be creating antonym word finds. (This is similar to Activity 2 of List 1 on synonyms.)

The puzzles are to contain at least twelve words. The shape of the puzzles may vary; however, simple squares or rectangles usually work best. Graph paper will facilitate the making of the puzzles. The words to be found may run from left to right, right to left, upward, downward, or diagonally.

A word bank is to be at the bottom of the puzzle. Rather than the words of the puzzle, however, the word bank is to include antonyms of the puzzle words. Students may use the antonyms from List 2, or they may use their own words.

You may wish to make copies of the completed word finds and allow students to work them out, or you may compile the puzzles in a class *Antonym Word Find Book*.

See List 1, Synonyms.

List 2. Antonyms

Antonyms are words that have opposite or approximately opposite meanings. Sometimes authors can find the precise word they need by thinking of its opposite first. Following are common antonyms. You can find many more by consulting your dictionary or thesaurus.

above — below	crowded — empty
add — subtract	curiosity — indifference
after — before	curtail — increase
alive — dead	day — night
all — none	defeat — victory
allow — prohibit	downcast — happy
answer — question	dull — bright
apart — together	even — odd
ask — tell	fast — slow
away — toward	father — mother
back — front	find — lose
ban — approve	first — last
barbaric — civilized	forbid — permit
bashful — bold	friend — enemy
beautiful — ugly	gentle — brutal
begin — end	good — bad
bored — enthusiastic	great — small
breezy — calm	group — individual
child — adult	hard — soft
closed — open	help — hurt
cold — hot	hero — villain
costly — cheap	hide — reveal
create — destroy	high — low
critic — supporter	kind — cruel
crooked — straight	knowledge — ignorance

leave — arrive

left — right

life — death

light — dark

little — big

long — short

loose — tight

many — few

mean — kind

more — less

move — stay

much — little

nasty — nice

near — far

neat — messy

neglect — cherish

nervous — calm

never — always

nothing — everything

now — then

obscure — clear

often — seldom

other — same

part — whole

positive — negative

problem — solution

proud — humble

right — wrong

safe — dangerous

same — different

shallow — deep

small — large

smooth — rough

start — stop

strong — weak

take — give

tall — short

that — this

there — here

to — from

under — over

up — down

wealthy — poor

young — old

3

HOMOGRAPHS

Teaching Suggestions

Many words in the English language have multiple meanings, and homographs are a special group of these words. Homographs are words that have the same spelling but different meanings and origins. Sometimes their pronunciations vary as well. While this may not present a major problem in writing (*līv* and *liv* are both spelled *live*), emphasize that homographs can cause slip-ups when students give a speech or presentation.

Use the word invalid (in-val'-id) as an example. If a student is giving a talk on acid rain, he or she might conclude that some of the theories of how acid rain forms are in-val'-id. However, if the student says they are in'-val-id, he or she is likely to draw chuckles instead of serious consideration.

ACTIVITY 1 — WORKSHEET 3–1, "THE CONCERT"

Objectives:

1. Students are to select the correct homographs in a given story.
2. Students are to write a personal account of a time they were surprised.

Procedure:

Hand out List 3 and discuss homographs. Next, distribute Worksheet 3–1 and instruct your students to read the story. They are to choose the correct homograph, based on its pronunciation, from the pairs of words. When students have completed the worksheet, you may wish to go over it orally with them.

Answer Key:

līv, rek' erd, prez' ent, min' it, lēd, clōs, wīnd, kon tent'
You can easily use the concept of the story "The Concert," which follows the list, to launch your students into a writing assignment. Ask them to think of a time they were surprised. What was the event? Instruct them to write a descriptive paragraph of this event. Encourage them to answer the questions who, what, when, where, why and how in their compositions.
See List 4, Homophones; and List 7, Easily Confused Words.

List 3. Homographs

Words that are spelled the same but have different meanings and origins are homographs. In many cases, homographs have the same pronunciation. *Bear* (bār), the animal, is pronounced the same as *bear* (bār), which means "to carry." Some homographs, however, are pronounced differently. *Invalid* (in' va lid), meaning "a bedridden person," is spoken with the accent on the first syllable, while *invalid* (in val' id), meaning "not valid," has the accent on the second syllable. The following list offers a varied assortment of some of the more common homographs of the English language, including pronunciations for those that are spoken differently.

angle — to fish with rod, line, and hook

angle — a point at which two straight lines meet

arms — limbs extending from shoulders to hands

arms — weapons

August (aw' gust) — the eighth month of the year

august (aw gust') — inspiring admiration

ball — a round object

ball — a formal dance

bank — the edge of a stream or lake

bank — a long mound or heap (snow, ground, etc.)

bank — a place where financial transactions are conducted

bear — to support or carry

bear — a large animal

boil — to bring to a seething, bubbling state by heating

boil — a local inflammation of the skin

buck — a male deer

buck — a dollar (slang)

chop — to cut

chop — the jaw of an animal

close (klōz) — to shut

close (klōs) — nearby

content (kon tent') — pleased, satisfied

content (kon' tent) — that which is contained

count — a title of nobility

count — to number

cue — a signal

cue — a long, tapering stick used in game of pool

date — the time of an event

date — a sweet fruit of the Eastern date palm

duck — a coarse cloth used for small sails and clothing

duck — to dip suddenly

duck — a broad-beaked, web-footed water bird

fan — a machine used to produce currents of air

fan — a devoted admirer (from *fanatic*)

flat — level

flat — a small apartment

13

fresh — new
fresh — disrespectful

grave — a burial site
grave — of great importance

hamper — a large covered basket or container
hamper — to hinder the movement of

haze — a light suspension of particles in the air
haze — to subject to pranks

invalid (in′ va lid) — a bedridden person
invalid (in val′ id) — not valid

jar — a container of glass or earthenware
jar — to cause to vibrate by sudden impact

kind — friendly, sympathetic
kind — a class or grouping

lark — to play or frolic
lark — a small bird

like — similar
like — to be pleased with

minute (min′ it) — sixty seconds
minute (mī nüt) — very small

moor — a marshy wasteland
moor — to secure a ship by anchors or cables

nag — an old horse
nag — to scold

pitcher — a container for pouring liquids
pitcher — a baseball player

quack — the sound of a duck
quack — one who pretends to have skill in medicine

rash — hasty
rash — an eruption on the skin

ray — a narrow beam of light
ray — a flat fish

saw — past tense of *see*
saw — a hand tool for cutting

school — a group of fish
school — an institution for learning

sock — a short stocking
sock — to hit hard

spell — a period of time
spell — an enchantment
spell — to say or write the letters of a word

tear (tēr) — a drop of fluid from the eye
tear (tār) — to rip apart

tire — to become weary
tire — a hoop of rubber placed around a wheel

wake — to rouse from sleep
wake — waves following a ship

wind (wind) — moving air
wind (wīnd) — to turn or twist around

yard — a measure of length equal to three feet
yard — an area surrounding a building

NAME _____   DATE _____

THE CONCERT

DIRECTIONS: Read the following story and circle the correct homographs from the pairs of words.

We went to a concert last night. We saw my favorite group (liv, līv). I have every single (rek′ erd, ri kord′) they ever made. It was the biggest surprise of my life when my parents gave me the tickets for a birthday (prez′ ent, pri zent′).

As the day of the concert approached, it seemed that I counted every (mī′ nüt, min′ it). When the day finally arrived, we left home early because there were no reserved seats.

As soon as we got to the concert, which was held in a park, I took the (led, lēd) and went directly to the main gate. I wanted to get as (clōs, clōz) to the front as possible. I tried to (wind, wīnd) my way to the stage, but it was too crowded. We had to settle toward the back, but I was (kon tent′, kon′ tent) to simply listen to the music.

4

HOMOPHONES

Teaching Suggestions

Homophones are words that have the same sound but different spellings and meanings. They are easy to misuse, and they creep into all forms of writing. Becoming familiar with common homophones is the best way to avoid making mistakes with them.

ACTIVITY — WORKSHEET 4–1, "JENNIFER'S PARTY"

Objectives:

1. Students are to select the correct homophones in a given story.
2. Students are to write an ending to a given story.

Procedure:

Distribute copies of List 4 and discuss homophones. Next, hand out copies of Worksheet 4–1. Instruct your students to read the partial story on the worksheet and circle the correct homophones from the pairs of words. When the students have completed the worksheet, you may wish to go over it orally.

Answer Key:

allowed, wait, knew, pray, hair, eight, patience, clothes, weather, break.

After the students have finished the first part of the activity, ask them how they would feel if they were Jennifer and had planned a special event and the weather threatened to spoil it. Ask if something like this has ever happened to any of them. If it has, ask for volunteers to share their experiences.

Next, instruct your students to write an ending to the story. Remind them to pay close attention to their use of homophones.

See List 3, Homographs; and List 7, Easily Confused Words.

List 4. Homophones

Homophones are words that have identical pronunciations but different spellings and meanings. They are easy to misuse. The following list contains some of the most common homophones.

air — the atmosphere

heir — a successor to property or rank

allowed — permitted

aloud — with a loud voice

altar — a raised structure for worship

alter — to change

ate — past tense of *eat*

eight — a number

ball — a round object

bawl — to cry or shout

base — the bottom part

bass — the lowest pitched male singing voice

be — to exist

bee — a flying insect

blew — past tense of *blow*

blue — the color of the clear daytime sky

bough — a tree limb

bow — the forward part of a ship

brake — a device for slowing or stopping a vehicle

break — to shatter or fracture

buy — to purchase

by — close or near

bye — short for *goodbye*

capital — money that is available for investment

capitol — the building in which a state government meets

cell — the fundamental unit of life

sell — to trade for money

cent — a hundredth part of a dollar

scent — a smell

sent — past tense of *send*

cereal — a food made from grains

serial — a story presented in installments

chews — to bite and crush with teeth (third-person form)

choose — to select

chord — a combination of tones sounded together

cord — a thick string or thin rope

cite — to bring forth as proof

sight — the ability to perceive with the eyes

site — a place

coarse — rough

course — the way covered

council — an assembly

counsel — to give advice

dear — highly valued

deer — an animal

dual — two

duel — combat between two persons

earn — to gain something through work

urn — a container

fir — a type of evergreen tree

fur — the hair covering the body of some animals

flea — a tiny insect

flee — to run away

flew — past tense of *fly*

flu — the short form of *influenza*, a viral infection

flue — a duct in a chimney

forth — forward in place or time

fourth — next after third

foul — filthy

fowl — a domesticated bird (chickens, ducks, geese)

hair — a filament growing from the skin of an animal

hare — a rabbit

hangar — a building for storing airplanes

hanger — a device from which to hang something

heal — to restore to health

heel — the back part of the bottom of the foot

he'll — contraction for *he will*

hear — to perceive with the ear

here — in this spot

heard — past tense of *hear*

herd — a group of animals

hi — a greeting

hie — to hurry

high — far up, tall

hoarse — harsh or husky sounding

horse — a large animal

hole — an opening

whole — entire, complete

hour — sixty minutes

our — belonging to us

knew — past tense of *know*

new — not existing before

knight — a soldier of feudal times

night — the time of darkness between daylight and sunset

know — to be aware of

no — a negative reply

lead — a heavy metal

led — past tense of *lead*, meaning "to guide"

lessen — to decrease

lesson — something to be learned

loan — to lend, or something that is lent

lone — solitary, single

made — past tense of *make*

maid — a female domestic servant

main — of great importance

Maine — a Northeastern state

mane — the long hair on the neck of an animal

might — power, strength

mite — a small insect

not — in no way

knot — an intertwining of rope or string

18

oar — a wooden lever used to propel a boat

or — a conjunction that introduces an alternative

ore — a mineral deposit

one — the lowest cardinal number

won — past tense of *win*

pail — a bucket

pale — faint in color

patience — the ability to endure things calmly

patients — people being treated for health problems

peace — calmness

piece — a part

peal — to ring

peel — to remove a covering

peer — an equal

pier — a dock

pray — to worship

prey — an animal hunted and killed for food

principal — most important in rank

principle — a fundamental law or truth

rain — condensed moisture falling from clouds

reign — the period during which a ruler maintains authority

rein — a leather strap used to control a horse

read — past tense of *read*

red — the color of blood

right — proper

rite — a religious practice

write — to set down in letters or words on paper

root — part of a plant that grows underground

route — a course or way

sail — a sheet of canvas used to catch the wind to move a boat

sale — an exchange of goods or services for money

sane — having a sound mind

seine — an open net used for fishing

sea — an ocean

see — to perceive with the eyes

sew — to mend

so — in such manner

sow — to plant

slay — to kill

sleigh — a large sled, typically drawn by horses

soar — to fly high

sore — painful

sole — the flat bottom part of the foot

soul — the spiritual part of a human being

some — a part of

sum — a total

son — a male child

sun — the star around which the earth revolves

stake — a sharpened stick or post

steak — a slice of beef

stationary — stable, not moving

stationery — writing paper

steal — to rob

steel — a strong metal made by mixing carbon and iron

straight — passing from one point directly to another

strait — a narrow channel of water joining two bodies of water

symbol — something that represents something else

cymbal — a musical instrument

tail — a flexible extension of an animal's spine

tale — a story

team — a group of people working together for a common goal

teem — to be stocked to overflowing

their — possessive pronoun meaning "of them"

there — in that place

they're — contraction for *they are*

to — preposition expressing motion toward

too — also

two — the sum of one and one

vain — conceited

vane — a device that shows the direction of the wind

vein — a blood vessel

waist — the part of the body below the ribs and above the hips

waste — to use foolishly

wait — to stay

weight — the amount of heaviness

ware — an article of merchandise

wear — to carry clothes on one's body

where — at what place

weak — feeble

week — seven successive days

weather — atmospheric conditions at a given place and time

whether — if

which — who or what one

witch — a woman who practices sorcery

who's — contraction for *who is*

whose — possessive pronoun meaning "of whom"

your — possessive form of *you*

you're — contraction for *you are*

NAME _____ DATE _____

JENNIFER'S PARTY

DIRECTIONS: Read the following story and circle the correct homophones from the pairs of words.

Jennifer's mother (allowed, aloud) Jennifer to have a party for her birthday. Jennifer could hardly (wait, weight).

"Oh, Mom," she said. "It's going to be great. I just hope it doesn't snow. You know how bad February can be."

"That's true," said her mother, "but it can just as easily be a nice day."

Unfortunately for Jennifer, when the day of her party came, the sky was cloudy and the forecast called for snow. Looking out the window at the dark clouds, Jennifer just (new, knew) her party would be ruined. She started to (prey, pray) for the sun to come out.

"Mom, what will we do if it snows and no one comes?" she said as she combed her (hare, hair).

"Your friends will come," her mother said.

"Well, I just wish it were (eight, ate) o'clock already and everybody was here," Jennifer said.

"You must have (patients, patience)," her mother said, smiling.

As Jennifer put on her party (clothes, close), the snow began. The (whether, weather) report said that it was likely to snow all night.

"Oh, no," Jennifer said, ready to (break, brake) into tears.

5

HARD-TO-SPELL WORDS (INTERMEDIATE)

Teaching Suggestions

Spelling in the English language is best described as inconsistent. Whereas some words are spelled the way they sound, many are not. Even when you follow spelling rules, you are confronted by exceptions. Nevertheless, spelling is an important subject. Correct spelling is essential to written communication, and questions on spelling appear on standardized and classroom tests.

You can utilize List 5 in several ways. Since many of the words listed appear on standardized tests, you might use them to augment your regular spelling assignments in preparation for testing. You can take sections of ten, fifteen, or twenty words each week and have your students learn their spellings and meanings. You can then test the students yourself or have them test each other by asking each other the words.

Aside from having your students memorize words and spelling rules, encourage them to incorporate the new words in their writing and speaking. This will help them to expand their vocabularies. In addition, you might suggest that they maintain lists of words that they find hard to spell (see Activity 2). Finally, encourage them to consult dictionaries whenever they are unsure of the correct spelling of a word.

ACTIVITY 1 — A TIME WHEN I WAS REALLY ANGRY

Objective:

Students are to write an account of a time they were angry; they are to use at least twenty of the words of List 5.

Procedure:

Hand out copies of List 5 and briefly review it, familiarizing your students with the hard-to-spell words. Next, ask the students if they have ever been angry. Certainly every hand should go up. Now ask them to think of a specific time when they were angry. What caused the incident? Who were the people involved? What happened? How was the matter finally resolved? Instruct them to write an account of this event, including what caused it and what happened. In their accounts they are to use at least twenty words of List 5.

ACTIVITY 2 — MAINTAINING PERSONAL SPELLING LISTS

Objective:

Students are to develop and maintain personal spelling lists of hard-to-spell words.

Procedure:

After distributing and briefly reviewing List 5, explain that most people have trouble with spelling. Indeed, many of us regularly misspell the same words. Maintaining personal lists of words we find particularly hard to spell can be helpful.

Instruct your students to set aside a few pages of loose-leaf paper (obtaining a small notebook is a good idea for this) and write down any words that they find hard to spell. Emphasize that they should write the words in rough alphabetical order, leaving plenty of space between so that more words can be included later.

When students are writing, they should keep List 5 as well as their personal spelling lists handy and refer to them as necessary.

See List 6, Hard-to-Spell Words (Advanced); and List 9, Compound Words.

List 5. Hard-to-Spell Words (Intermediate)

All of us have trouble spelling some words. However, many people tend to misspell the same words. Keeping a list of hard-to-spell words like these handy can help you avoid spelling mistakes in your writing.

absence	country	guess	once
address	county	Halloween	opinion
adjust	cousin	hamburger	opposite
advise	cruel	handkerchief	outside
again	decorate	handle	party
all right	describe	haven't	patient
along	desperate	headquarters	peace
a lot	didn't	heard	people
already	diet	height	piece
although	different	hello	please
arithmetic	distance	history	plumber
autumn	distribute	hospital	poem
awhile	doctor	hour	poison
bacon	doubt	house	popular
bakery	doughnut	immediately	practice
balloon	early	instead	pretty
because	emergency	its	principal
been	employ	it's	principle
believe	enough	knew	profession
birthday	entrance	know	quarter
bought	envelope	laid	quiet
break	erosion	language	quit
brought	excellent	latter	quite
budget	exhale	little	raise
built	exist	loose	read
children	exit	loving	receive
chocolate	experience	magic	remember
choose	favorite	maybe	respect
close	February	memory	rhyme
closet	fierce	minute	right
collect	first	morning	rough
comfortable	fourth	motor	route
compare	friend	mysterious	sandwich
continent	fuel	neither	Saturday
cough	galaxy	none	schedule
could	getting	o'clock	school
couldn't	guard	often	separate

several
shoes
since
sincerely
skiing
skis
something
sometimes
soon
steak
straight
studying
substitute
sugar
summer
Sunday

suppose
surely
surface
surprise
surround
swimming
teacher
telescope
terrible
Thanksgiving
their
themselves
there
they'll
they're
though

thought
through
tired
together
tomorrow
tonight
too
traveling
trouble
truly
Tuesday
universe
until
vacant
vacation
vegetable

victim
wear
weather
Wednesday
weigh
were
we're
when
where
which
whole
write
wrote
yield
your
you're

6

HARD-TO-SPELL WORDS (ADVANCED)

Teaching Suggestions

As the words of the English language become longer, they generally become harder to spell. Students (and adults) are regularly confused by silent vowels, dropped letters, consonant blends that defy the logic of pronunciation (*gh* in *laugh* and *ph* in *phone,* for instance), and some words that are not spoken at all as they should be, such as *colonel.* Along with the words of List 6, it is not unusual for advanced students to have trouble with some of the words of the intermediate list, and you should use both these lists according to the needs of your class.

While teaching spelling to students, you must keep in mind that some students are and always will be weak spellers. Moreover, avoid linking poor spelling with general intelligence or the ability to write well; Ernest Hemingway was a notoriously bad speller. Your purpose should be to help your students realize that if they have a spelling problem, they can take steps to compensate for it.

One step, obviously, is to encourage students to use the dictionary, not just for class but whenever they are unsure of the correct spelling of a word. Another step is to urge students to make a list of words that they find particularly vexing. Third, you can stress that by careful editing, there need be few, if any, spelling mistakes on any written work.

ACTIVITY 1 — MY DREAM DATE

Objectives:

1. Students are to write a story about a fantasy date with a celebrity of their choice.
2. Students are to act as editors and proofread a partner's composition for spelling errors.

Procedure:

Ask your students to imagine this situation: They have a date, a real night on the town, with any celebrity they wish. Who would they choose?

Instruct them to write about their dream date. Why did they choose this person? Where did they go? What did they talk about? What did they do? If one of your students claims that he or she has no dream date, you can open the assignment up to spending a date with a professional athlete, politician, or religious leader.

When students have completed their drafts, instruct them to exchange their stories with a partner. Partners then act as editors and proofread the stories, circling any spelling mistakes. You may distribute Lists 5 and 6 to help editors with their proofreading. You should also suggest that editors consult a dictionary if doubtful about a word.

After the papers are returned, the writers should correct the spelling mistakes and then go on to completing the final copy.

Extension:

You can extend this activity by using it as a springboard for students to develop personal spelling lists. Students should list, in rough alphabetical order, words that they find difficult to spell. They can do this in a notebook or on looseleaf paper, and should leave space between words so that they can add new words. New words will be added with subsequent writing assignments. The personal spelling lists should be handy for reference during every writing assignment.

ACTIVITY 2 — SPELLING BEE WITH A TWIST

Objective:

Students are to participate in a spelling bee.

Procedure:

Divide your class into groups of two or three. Groups act as one person during the spelling bee. Older students may at first be amused by this idea, but as you explain the rules, their interest and sense of competition will likely be stimulated.

Compile enough words so that each group has five opportunities to spell words. Thus, if you have ten groups, you will need at least fifty different words. You may use the words from Lists 5 or 6 as well as words from your class reading or spelling vocabulary. The words should be new to the students, however, and should be at the upper levels of their vocabularies. This is the reason for the teams. Because the words are new, students will have the chance to confer to decide on the correct spelling.

Start by saying the first word twice to group one. You may repeat it once if necessary. The members of the group then have some time to decide on the correct spelling. You might decide to limit this time to thirty seconds. If the group spells the word incorrectly, move on to the next word and the next group. Using a new word prevents the next group from having additional time to decide on the correct spelling. Note: Even though the first group got their word wrong, they are still in the game. When the second group is done, go on to the next group and so on.

Points are scored by spelling a word correctly, one point for each word. At the end of the round (each team having had a chance to spell five words), you can take the top two or three teams and have a playoff. You should have a fresh list of words for this. You might need five or six words for each team before a winner is declared.

If your school has a school newspaper or a PTA newsletter, be sure that the names of the winners are included in the next issue. You might also put the names of the winners on a bulletin board in a Winner's Circle Display.

This activity can generate much enthusiasm. It offers students the opportunity to have fun with spelling, while underscoring the importance of spelling correctly.

See List 5, Hard-to-Spell Words (Intermediate); and List 9, Compound Words.

List 6. Hard-to-Spell Words (Advanced)

The words in the following list are often misspelled by students and adults. Unfortunately, these words are used frequently in routine written communication. Having this list nearby when writing can help you reduce your spelling errors.

acceptable	category	disease	insufficient
accommodate	cemetery	distinction	intelligent
accustom	colonel	dominant	interest
ache	colossal	dubious	interpretation
achieve	commemorate	dynamic	interrupt
acquire	committee	endeavor	invigorate
adolescent	comparative	effective	irrelevant
advantageous	concede	efficient	itinerant
advice	conceive	embarrass	jealousy
aisle	condemn	emigrate	journalist
amateur	condense	enigmatic	jubilant
analyze	conscience	environment	justification
anticipate	conscientious	especially	license
antidote	conscious	exaggerate	lieutenant
anxiety	consequence	except	literal
apparent	controversy	exercise	logical
appetizer	council	existence	magnificent
appreciate	counsel	familiar	majestic
apprehension	counterfeit	fascinate	maneuver
arctic	courtesy	foreseeable	marriage
argument	criticize	gaiety	mathematics
arrange	definitely	gauge	medicine
athlete	delectable	generous	mediocre
attentive	deliberate	grammar	merit
audible	descendant	guarantee	meticulous
augment	descent	guidance	miniature
authority	description	hesitate	miscellaneous
autonomy	desert	immune	mischief
awkward	despondent	impartial	muscle
bargain	dessert	important	necessary
bellow	dignity	impressive	niece
beneficial	dilemma	improbable	noticeable
bilingual	diligence	impulsive	obscure
breathe	disagree	incorruptible	occasion
briny	disastrous	incredible	occurrence
business	discipline	indecision	opportunity
calendar	disclose	informative	optimism

opulence
parallel
paralyze
particular
perceptible
perform
personnel
pessimism
politics
possession
possible
prejudice
prescription
prestige
prevalent
privilege

probably
procedure
professor
prolong
prominent
propensity
pummel
pursue
receipt
recommend
repetition
restaurant
reverberate
rhythm
saucer
seize

sergeant
significant
similar
sophomore
spacious
stationary
subtle
succeed
sultry
supersede
susceptible
technique
territory
thorough
transferred
translucent

transparent
turmoil
unnecessary
urgent
vacuum
validation
valuable
variegate
vengeance
verdict
vigor
villain
visible
wrath
wrench
yacht

7

EASILY CONFUSED WORDS

Teaching Suggestions

There are many words in the English language that sound so much alike that they are easily confused. How many times have you seen *affect* and *effect* interchanged? What about *capital* and *capitol*? *Its* and *it's*? If you are like most teachers, you have probably circled mistakes like these far more than you would like to remember.

Since there is no set of rules that you can give your students to use the words of List 7 correctly, your teaching strategy should focus on making your students aware of these words and encouraging them to consult dictionaries whenever they are doubtful of a specific usage.

The following activity will help your students become familiar with common, easily confused words.

ACTIVITY — WORKSHEET 7–1, "SPACEMAN IN THE BACKYARD"

Objectives:

1. Given a story containing pairs of easily confused words, students are to choose the correct word in each pair.
2. Students are to write an imaginary account of a meeting with an alien.

Procedure:

Distribute copies of List 7 and review it, familiarizing your students with easily confused words. Emphasize that these words are often interchanged, even though their meanings are quite different.

Next, hand out copies of Worksheet 7–1. Instruct your students to read the story and circle the correct word from the pairs of easily confused words. You may permit students to use List 7 or a dictionary.

When students have completed the worksheet, you may wish to go over it orally and answer any questions they might have.

Answer Key:

where, illusion, which, four, assistance, It's, Then, device, here, right.

For the next part of this assignment, ask your students to imagine that they have met an alien. To stimulate their thinking, ask the following questions: Where did they meet him/her/it? How did they communicate? What did they say? Did the alien speak English? What happened? Did the alien return to his/her/its home planet?

Instruct your students to write an imaginary story about their meeting with an alien. Remind them to pay close attention to any easily confused words they may use in their stories.

See List 3, Homographs; and List 4, Homophones.

List 7. Easily Confused Words

Because it has borrowed from so many other languages, the English language is one of the richest in the world. We have words for just about everything. We have homographs, words that are spelled alike but have different meanings. We have homophones, words that sound alike but have different meanings. And we have words that simply sound similar. All of this of course makes a maddening assortment of easily confused words, of which some of the most common follow.

accede — to agree
exceed — to go beyond the limit

accept — to receive
except — to leave out

access — a way of approach
excess — that which surpasses a limit

ad — an advertisement
add — to find the sum of

advice — an offered opinion
advise — to give advice to

affect — to act upon
effect — a result

alley — a passageway between buildings
alloy — a mixture of two or more metals

ally — to form an alliance

allot — to divide according to shares
a lot — many

allowed — permitted
aloud — with a loud voice

all ready — everything is set
already — before this

angel — a heavenly spirit
angle — a figure formed by two straight lines diverging from a common point

annual — yearly
annul — to void

ascent — the act of rising or climbing
assent — to agree

assistance — help
assistants — helpers

attendance — the act of being present
attendants — people who are present, usually to serve

band — a group of musicians
banned — prohibited

bare — without covering
bear — a large animal

bell — an object that gives a clear, musical note when struck
belle — a beautiful woman

beside — at the side of
besides — in addition

between — in the middle of two
among — mixed with

bibliography — a list of articles or books about a subject
biography — an account of a person's life

bizarre — odd or strange
bazaar — a fair

board — a long plank of wood
bored — not interested

born — to have been brought forth
borne — carried

borough — a town
burro — a donkey
burrow — a hole in the ground
    dug by an animal
bough — a tree limb
bow — to bend the body as a sign
    of respect
bouillon — broth
bullion — uncoined gold or silver
brake — a device to stop a vehicle
break — to shatter
breath — air taken into the lungs
breathe — to inhale and exhale air
canvas — coarse cloth
canvass — to examine an area
    thoroughly
capital — money that is available
    for investment
capitol — the building in which a
    state government meets
casual — a relaxed, easy manner
causal — relating to a cause
chord — a combination of three or
    more musical tones
cord — thick string or rope
cite — to bring forth as proof
sight — the ability to perceive
    with the eyes
site — a place
close — to shut
clothes — wearing apparel
coarse — rough
course — the way covered
colonel — a military rank
kernel — the inner portion
coma — a deep sleep caused by
    sickness or by injury to the
    brain
comma — a punctuation mark
complement — something that
    completes another thing
compliment — a flattering
    comment

confidant — a person in whom one
    can confide
confident — self-assured
conscience — knowledge or sense
    of what is right and wrong
conscious — being aware of one's
    surroundings
council — an assembly
counsel — to give advice
country — a nation
county — a division of a state
decent — proper
descent — the act of coming down
desert — a dry wasteland
dessert — food served at the end of
    a meal
device — something built for a
    specific plan
devise — to invent or scheme
doe — a female deer
dough — a moistened flour
    mixture used in baking
dual — two
duel — combat between two people
elicit — to draw out
illicit — unlawful
emerge — to rise out of
immerse — to plunge into
emigrate — to leave one's country
    to settle in another
immigrate — to come into another
    country to settle
eminent — high in rank
imminent — threatening to occur
    immediately
envelop — to surround
envelope — the cover of a letter
expand — to increase in size
expend — to consume by use
faint — to pass out, a weakness, to
    swoon
feint — a deceptive move

farther — to a greater distance

further — in addition to

fewer — smaller in number

less — not as much

flair — a talent or ability

flare — to burn brightly

foreword — the introduction to a book

forward — movement toward a place in front

formally — in a standard or conventional manner

formerly — earlier in time

forth — forward in place or time

fourth — next after third

hangar — a building for storing airplanes

hanger — a device from which to hang something

hear — to perceive with the ear

here — this place

heard — past tense of *hear*

herd — a group of animals

hole — an opening

whole — entire, complete

human — a person

humane — kind, benevolent

idle — inactive

idol — an image of a god

illusion — an unreal image

allusion — an indirect hint or suggestion

in — within, inside of

into — motion toward a point inside

its — a possessive pronoun

it's — contraction for *it is*

knew — past tense of *know*

new — not existing before

know — to be aware of

no — not any

later — coming afterward

latter — the second of two

lay — to place or put down

lie — to be in a reclined position

lead — a heavy metal

led — past tense of *lead* meaning "to guide"

least — smallest

lest — for fear that

lessen — to decrease

lesson — something to be learned

lightening — to make less heavy

lightning — a flash of light caused by the discharge of atmospheric electricity

loose — not tight

lose — to be deprived of

meat — flesh used for food

meet — to encounter

medal — an award

metal — a mineral substance characterized by malleability

moral — ethical, virtuous

morale — strong spirit in the face of emergency

of — belonging to; from

off — away

passed — having gone beyond

past — of a former time

patience — the ability to endure things calmly

patients — people being treated for health problems

pedal — a device used to transmit the power of the foot

peddle — to go from place to place selling things

personal — pertaining to a particular individual

personnel — people employed by a business or office

picture — a drawing

pitcher — a container for pouring liquids

pitcher — a baseball player

plain — vast, flat land

plane — short for *airplane*

precede — to go before

proceed — to move onward

principal — most important in rank

principle — a fundamental law or truth

quiet — still, without noise

quit — to give up

quite — completely

rain — condensed moisture falling from clouds

reign — the period during which a ruler maintains authority

rein — a leather strap used to control a horse

road — track or way for travelers

rode — past tense of *ride*

role — a part played by an actor

roll — to turn over and over; to move on wheels

sole — the flat part of the foot

soul — the spiritual part of a human being

stake — a sharpened stick or post

steak — a slice of beef

straight — passing from one point directly to another

strait — a narrow channel of water joining two bodies of water

than — a conjunction that denotes comparison

then — at that time

their — possessive pronoun meaning "of them"

there — in that place

they're — contraction for *they are*

threw — past tense of *throw*

through — going in at one end and emerging from the other

to — preposition expressing motion toward

too — also

two — the sum of one and one

veracious — truthful

voracious — extremely hungry

waist — the part of the human body below the ribs and above the hips

waste — to expend uselessly

wait — to stay

weight — the amount of heaviness

ware — an article of merchandise

were — past tense of the verb *be*

where — at what place

weather — atmospheric conditions at a given place and time

whether — in case; if it be the case that

which — who or what one

witch — a woman who practices sorcery

who's — contraction for *who is*

whose — possessive pronoun meaning "of whom"

your — possessive form of *you*

you're — contraction for *you are*

NAME _____   DATE _____

SPACEMAN IN THE BACKYARD

DIRECTIONS: Read the following story and circle the correct word from each pair of words. Be careful. The words are easily confused.

The crash in the backyard startled Bobby. He jumped up from the couch (where, were) he was reading and hurried to the back window. He rubbed his eyes. Was it an (allusion, illusion)?

Quickly he went outside. The rocket, (which, witch) was about (four, for) feet long, was stuck front first in the ground. When Bobby bent close to it, he heard a squeaky voice.

"Earthling, I need your (assistance, assistants)."

"What?" said Bobby, astonished.

"Open the hatch," the voice said. "(Its, It's) stuck."

Bobby pulled on the small door until it popped open. A little man climbed out.

"Thank you," he said. "May I use your phone?"

"My phone?" said Bobby.

"How else can I call for a tow-craft?" said the alien.

"Right, sure," said Bobby. (Then, Than) he carried the spaceman inside.

Bobby put the little alien next to the telephone. The alien took a tiny (devise, device) and placed it against the receiver. "Taps into the phone company's computers," he explained. After he was done speaking in a strange language to someone, he put his instrument away. "They'll be (here, hear) any minute," he said to Bobby.

He was (right, write). In a few minutes, the tow-craft came and took hold of his disabled ship.

"Thanks for everything!" he said as he climbed aboard and left.

8

SOUND WORDS

Teaching Suggestions

The use of words that sound like what they describe is known as onomatopoeia. Sound words can effectively add interest and freshness to writing and make it come alive for readers.

When a writer describes rumbling thunder, crackling fire, or a sizzling, juicy steak, the reader's mind conjures up powerful mental images in which he or she sees as well as hears the action. Students should be made aware of how sound words can enhance their writing significantly.

ACTIVITY 1 — SOUND POEMS

Objective:

Students are to write poems that focus on a sound or sounds.

Procedure:

Distribute copies of List 8. Give your students a few moments to look over the list, then ask for volunteers to take a sound word and match it with an action. Offer these examples: donkeys bray, wolves howl, old floors creak, and leaves rustle. Have your students name several examples.

Next, explain that they are to select a sound or sounds and write a descriptive poem. Emphasize that poems may or may not rhyme and may or may not have a specific meter. The focus of the writing should be on the expression, not the conventions, of poetical form. Demanding that students utilize rhyme and meter may interfere with their creativity.

You may ask students to share their poems by reading them to the class, or you may compile them in a book entitled *Sound Poems*.

ACTIVITY 2 — A LISTENING ADVENTURE

Objective:

Students are to visit a place in which various sounds are apparent, and write a descriptive paragraph of this place.

Procedure:

Distribute copies of List 8 and review it with your students. Explain that through the effective use of sound words, writers can make scenes realistic. In order to write accurately about a place, many writers will go there to experience it firsthand. They carefully look at the area, noting the physical objects, and they also listen to the sounds of the place.

For this assignment, ask your students to pick a place in which various sounds are apparent. Offer these suggestions as examples: the school cafeteria, a busy city thoroughfare, a park, a shopping mall, a school basketball game. You might ask for students to volunteer some other places.

Instruct your students to visit for at least fifteen minutes the place they have chosen. They are to listen carefully and take notes of all the sounds they hear. When they return to class, they are to write a descriptive paragraph of the place they visited, detailing all the sounds they heard.

See List 10, Sensory Words.

List 8. Sound Words

Sound words, also known as onomatopoeic words, imitate the sounds they describe. Bees *buzz*, telephones *ring*, and cats *meow*. Effective use of sound words can enhance the imagery and realism of writing.

ack-ack	clomp	grind	quack	squeak
bang	cluck	growl	rap	squeal
beep	coo	grunt	rev	squish
bong	cough	hiss	ring	swish
boom	crack	honk	roar	tick
bowwow	crackle	hoot	rumble	thud
bray	crash	howl	rustle	thump
buzz	creak	hum	screech	tinkle
chirp	crunch	meow	shriek	twang
chug	cuckoo	moo	sizzle	whack
clack	ding-dong	neigh	slurp	whiz
clang	drip	ping	smack	whoop
clatter	fizz	plop	smash	zip
click	flap	pop	snort	zoom
clink	grate	puff	splash	

40

9

COMPOUND WORDS

Teaching Suggestions

Compound words are made up of two or more words that have evolved into a single meaning. It is easy to make mistakes with compound words. Frequently students and adults do not recognize compound words or don't know whether to combine, hyphenate, or leave a space between the words that make up the compound. Sometimes dictionaries don't agree either, which only adds to the overall mystery and confusion.

The best thing you can do for your students regarding compound words is to make them aware of these words and encourage them to consult a dictionary or stylebook whenever the slightest doubt arises. Proper use of compound words helps to make writing correct in a mechanical sense, which reflects positively on the author.

ACTIVITY 1 — WORKSHEET 9–1, "COOKIES FOR THE CLASS TRIP"

Objectives:

1. Students are to identify compound words in a given story.
2. Students are to write about a time they did something in which they were nervous or unsure of themselves.

Procedure:

Hand out copies of List 9 and discuss compound words with your students. Explain what they are and emphasize that they may be closed, hyphenated, or open.

Now distribute copies of Worksheet 9–1. Instruct your students to underline all compound words they find in the story. You may wish to permit them to use List 9 to find the compound words in the story. When everyone is finished, you can go over the worksheet orally. Remind your students that they should consult dictionaries or stylebooks when they are unsure about a compound word.

Answer Key:

everyone, all out, oatmeal, sidewalk, anything, everybody, weekend, wildflowers, sunshine, flowerpot, doorbell, heavyset, old-fashioned, All right

For the next part of the assignment, ask your students if, like the character in the story, they have ever done something during which they were nervous. Perhaps they had to sell something, handle an important responsibility, go for a job interview, or give a speech in front of the class. Instruct your students to write a descriptive account of this experience. Encourage them to describe what they did as well as how they felt and, of course, how things turned out. Remind them to pay close attention to any compound words they may use in their stories.

ACTIVITY 2 — HOW MANY CAN YOU FIND?

Objective:

Given a list of root words, students are to make as many compound words as they can.

Procedure:

Distribute copies of List 9 an discuss compound words with your class. For this activity, students may work alone, or you may divide them into teams of two. If you have an odd number in class, ask if someone would volunteer to work alone, or you may work with a student yourself.

Explain that you will give the class a list of root words and the students will be required to make as many compound words from these words as possible. The person or team with the most compound words wins. You may set a time limit of a class period if you wish or make it an overnight assignment. You may allow your students to use dictionaries.

Write the following word list on the board:

house	half	play
back	land	rain
day	out	way
down	one	head
light	man	walk

As incentive, you should offer a prize. While the incentive is up to you, something to consider is adding points to your students' last writing assignments. First place might earn 5 points, second place 3, and third place 2. You might also put the winners' names on a bulletin board, advertising their accomplishment, and display their list of compound words.

Answers will vary; as long as a word can be substantiated as correct in a dictionary or stylebook it should be counted as correct.

See List 5, Hard-to-Spell Works (Intermediate); and List 6, Hard-to-Spell Words (Advanced).

List 9. Compound Words

Compound words are words made by combining two or more words. Compound words may be joined, as in *drugstore*; connected by a hyphen, as in *drive-in*; or left open, as in *zoo keeper*. Fortunately, dictionaries are available to lessen the confusion.

able-bodied	blackout	custom-made	flashlight
above-ground	bloodhound	cutout	floodlight
afterthought	blood pressure	dark horse	flowerpot
air conditioning	bloodshot	darkroom	folklore
airline	bloodstream	daydream	football
airmail	blowup	daytime	free-for-all
airplane	blueprint	dishpan	frogman
airport	bookcase	dogcatcher	frostbite
all-American	bookkeeper	doghouse	gentleman
all out	bookmark	door knob	goldfish
all right	boxcar	double talk	goodbye
all-round	box seat	downfall	good-looking
all-time	breakdown	downpour	grasshopper
alma mater	breakneck	downstairs	haircut
alongside	broadcast	downtown	half brother
anchorman	brokenhearted	dragonfly	half sister
anchorwoman	brother-in-law	drive-in	halfway
anybody	bulldog	dropout	handcuff
anyhow	buttercup	drugstore	handlebar
anymore	buttermilk	dust bowl	hangup
anyone	campfire	dry clean	hard-boiled
ashtray	carpool	dry dock	hardware
backbone	checkmate	earring	haystack
back door	checkup	earthquake	headache
back talk	classmate	eyeball	headlight
backyard	classroom	eyelid	headline
badlands	clipboard	eye shadow	headquarters
bad-tempered	close call	fairy tale	highchair
barefoot	close-up	fallout	highrise
baseball	clothesline	farmland	high spirits
basketball	cold shoulder	far-reaching	highway
bathroom	copout	field glasses	holdup
battle-axe	copperhead	filmstrip	homemade
battleship	copyright	firehouse	homework
beanbag	cowboy	fireplace	horseshoe
birthday	cross-country	fishhook	household
birthplace	crosswalk	flagpole	housekeeper
blackboard	cupcake	flashback	infield

jellybean
jellyfish
landlady
landlord
landslide
lawn mower
leftover
lifeboat
lifeguard
lifeline
life-size
light-year
lockjaw
locksmith
lookout
loudspeaker
lukewarm
midnight
moonwalk
motorcycle
newsboy
newscast
newspaper
newsprint
nightgown
notebook
oatmeal
offbeat
old-fashioned
outboard
outcome
outcry
outfield
outfit
outlaws
out-of-bounds
outside
overalls

overcoat
overlook
overpass
paperback
password
payoff
peanut
peppermint
pickup
pigtail
pinball
pinpoint
playmate
playpen
ponytail
popcorn
postcard
postman
pushover
quicksand
railroad
railway
rainbow
raincoat
rattlesnake
redwood
ripoff
roadside
rowboat
runaway
runway
rush hour
safety glass
sailboat
sandpaper
scarecrow
school bus
screwball

self-made
shipwreck
shoelace
shortstop
sidewalk
silverware
skateboard
skyline
skyscraper
slipcover
snowdrift
snowfall
snowstorm
softball
spacecraft
speedboat
splashdown
spotlight
stagehand
stairway
stand-in
starfish
streetcar
suitcase
sunbeam
sunflower
sunshine
sweatshirt
sweetheart
teacup
teenager
textbook
thumbtack
thunderstorm
timeline
timetable
tiptoe
toenail

toothbrush
toothpick
touchdown
troublemaker
tugboat
turntable
turtleneck
undercover
underground
undertaker
uproot
uptown
volleyball
washcloth
washroom
wastebasket
watchdog
watchman
watercolor
waterfall
waterfront
watermelon
weatherman
weekday
weekend
well-to-do
whirlpool
wholesale
wildcat
wildflower
windmill
windpipe
windshield
woodland
woodpecker
wristwatch
zoo keeper

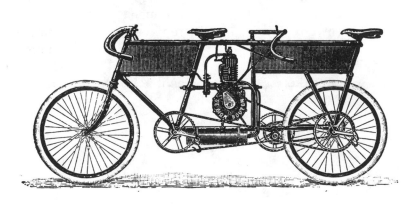

NAME _____   DATE _____

COOKIES FOR THE CLASS TRIP

DIRECTIONS: Read the following story and circle all the compound words.

Lori recalled when Mrs. Anderson told the class about their class trip. Everyone was excited. Even though it was still weeks away, Mrs. Anderson explained, they had to go all out and raise the money as soon as possible. Lori didn't know then that this would mean she would be selling oatmeal cookies.

Standing on the sidewalk before the small, brick house, Lori was nervous. She had never sold anything before. She was afraid of making a mistake and appearing foolish. But everybody had to do their part.

Lori took a deep breath and opened the gate. There are better ways to spend a weekend, she thought. As she walked toward the porch, she noticed that wildflowers filled the yard. They bloomed in the sunshine and swayed in the soft breeze like gentle waves. They were so pretty that Lori wasn't watching where she was going, and she almost tripped over a flowerpot by the steps.

She groaned at her clumsiness and rang the doorbell. In a moment, an elderly, heavyset woman with a friendly smile answered.

"Hello," said Lori. "I'm Lori Douglas from Central School. We're selling tasty, old-fashioned cookies to raise money for our class trip. Would you like to order some?" She offered the lady the catalog.

The woman paused a moment as she looked over the selections. "All right," she said. "Let me see. I can't resist cookies."

10

SENSORY WORDS

Teaching Suggestions

Sensory words are those words that appeal to the senses of sight, touch, hearing, smell, and taste. Because they can evoke strong mental images, they are essential to most forms of writing. Sensory words help a reader see and feel action.

Encourage your students to use sensory words in their writing, and point out the effective use of sensory words whenever possible in their reading books or textbooks. Make your students aware of how authors use sensory words to enhance their stories and articles.

ACTIVITY 1 — NOW FEELINGS

Objective:

Students are to write a composition describing their current feelings.

Procedure:

Distribute copies of List 10 and discuss sensory words with your students. Next, ask them how they feel today, right now. Are they happy? Sad? Nervous? Uncomfortable? Energetic? Why do they feel the way they do? Did they have an argument with a parent? Are they looking forward to a date? Or are they bored with your writing class? (There's always one. . . .)

Instruct your students to write a composition entitled "Now Feelings," in which they are to describe their feelings and offer reasons why they feel this way. Encourage them to use sensory words to sharpen their writing.

ACTIVITY 2 — IN THE EYE OF THE BEHOLDER

Objective:

Students are to select a person they know well and write a descriptive paragraph about that person.

Procedure:

Distribute copies of List 10 and discuss with your students the value of sensory words to writing. For this activity, ask them to select a person they know well but who is not in the room. They are to write a descriptive paragraph of this individual. Encourage them to use sensory words to make this person come alive to readers.

ACTIVITY 3 — IT'S SO GOOD . . .

Objective:

Students are to select one of their favorite foods and write a descriptive paragraph.

Procedure:

Hand out copies of List 10 and discuss with your students the importance of sensory words to writing. For this activity, ask them to pick one of their favorite foods or desserts. Instruct them to write a descriptive paragraph of it, using sensory words to enable their readers to smell and taste the delicious fare.

See List 8, Sound Words.

List 10. Sensory Words

Authors rely on sensory words to create strong imagery. Effective use of sensory words enables readers to *see* the fistfight between the hero and villain, *smell* the dank air of an ancient tomb, *feel* the heat of a raging fire, *hear* the winter wind blow, and *taste* the foods of a grand feast. The following lists of words that refer to the senses of sight, touch, hearing, smell, and taste can help you add realism to your writing.

SIGHT WORDS

angular	dark	homely	shiny
bent	deep	huge	short
big	dim	immense	skinny
billowy	distinct	light	small
black	dull	lithe	soaring
blonde	elegant	little	spotless
blushing	enormous	long	square
branching	fancy	low	steep
bright	fat	misty	stormy
brilliant	filthy	motionless	straight
broad	flat	muddy	strange
brunette	flickering	murky	sunny
bulky	fluffy	narrow	swooping
chubby	foggy	obtuse	tall
circular	forked	pale	tapering
clean	fuzzy	petite	translucent
cloudy	gigantic	portly	ugly
colorful	glamorous	quaint	unsightly
colossal	gleaming	radiant	unusual
contoured	glistening	rectangular	weird
craggy	globular	reddish	wide
crinkled	glowing	rippling	wiry
crooked	graceful	rotund	wispy
crowded	grotesque	shadowy	wizened
crystalline	hazy	shallow	
curved	high	sheer	
cute	hollow	shimmering	

TOUCH WORDS

breezy	cool	dirty	elastic
bumpy	cuddly	downy	filthy
chilly	damp	dry	fluffy
cold	dank	dusty	frosty

gooey	plastic	slippery	tender
greasy	prickly	slushy	tepid
gritty	rough	smooth	tight
hard	searing	sodden	uneven
hot	shaggy	soft	warm
icy	sharp	solid	waxen
loose	silky	sticky	wet
lukewarm	slick	stinging	wooden
melted	slimy	sweaty	

HEARING WORDS

bang	harsh	noisy	snarl
bark	haw	pealing	snort
boom	hiss	pop	softly
buzz	hoarse	purring	splash
coo	howl	quietly	squeak
crackling	hushed	raspy	squeal
crash	husky	reverberating	thud
crunching	lapping	rumble	thump
cry	loud	rustle	thundering
deafening	melodious	scream	tinkle
echoing	moan	screech	wail
faint	muffled	shriek	whimper
groan	mumble	shrill	whine
growl	murmur	sloshing	whisper
gurgling	mutter	snapping	whistling

SMELL WORDS

acrid	delicious	putrid	sour
antiseptic	fragrant	rancid	spicy
bitter	fresh	rich	stale
burning	medicinal	rotten	stinky
choking	musty	salty	strong
clean	pungent	smoky	sweet

TASTE WORDS

acidic	hot	salty	strong
bitter	juicy	savory	sweet
cool	mild	sour	tangy
creamy	nutty	spicy	tart
delicious	peppery	stale	tasteless
gooey	ripe	sticky	tasty

11

TIME WORDS

Teaching Suggestions

Time—we never seem to have enough of it; yet, for most people, it's something that is easy to waste. Indeed, many of us check our watches or clocks several times a day and still manage to be late.

Time is no less important for authors. Time words are essential to the setting of stories and articles. They also help clarify transitions, and they allow us to follow the sequence of a story more easily. This is not all they do, though. Imagine trying to characterize a person or object without using such basic time words as young or old. Or try to imagine a story evolving without time passing.

ACTIVITY 1 — A DIARY OF TODAY

Objective:

Students are to write a diary entry focusing on their actions during a one-day period.

Procedure:

Distribute copies of List 11 and discuss with your students the importance of time words to writing. For this activity, instruct them to write a diary entry of a day—from the time they wake in the morning until they go to sleep at night. Remind them to take note of the way they use time words to clarify their writing.

ACTIVITY 2 — AN AUTOBIOGRAPHICAL SKETCH

Objective:

Students are to select a part of their lives and write about it in an autobiographical sketch.

Procedure:

Distribute copies of List 11 and discuss with your students the importance of time words to writing. Next, review the features of an autobiographical sketch. It is a brief account of one's own life, generally focusing on one area, aspect, or accomplishment.

Ask your students to think of some area of their lives that they would like to share. This might be a particular skill, hobby, talent, or special experience. Then instruct them to write an autobiographical sketch. Remind them to notice how they use time words to develop their writing.

List 11. Time Words

Time is one of our most basic concepts. Without the understanding of time passing, tomorrow would never come. It is not surprising, therefore, that time words are fundamental to writing. Time words enable authors to plot stories from beginning to end. They also help to describe settings and characters.

adolescence	daylight	long	punctual
adulthood	decade	mature	quick
after	dusk	middle age	rapid
afternoon	early	midnight	recent
age	ending	millennium	recur
ancient	eons	minute	second
annual	episode	modern	semiannual
antiquity	epoch	moment	short
bedtime	era	morning	slowly
before	evening	new	speedy
beginning	extinct	night	sporadic
biannual	fast	noon	sunrise
bimonthly	fleeting	novel	sunset
brief	flying	obsolete	swift
century	historic	occasional	tardy
childhood	immature	old	teenage
constant	infancy	outdated	twilight
continual	instant	overdue	up-to-date
crawling	instantaneous	past	worn-out
current	interim	period	year
cyclical	intermittent	prehistoric	yearly
dawn	late	prior	young
day	lengthy	prompt	youth
daybreak			

Lists and Activities
for Nonfiction Writing

12

ADVERTISING WORDS

Teaching Suggestions

Each day we are bombarded by thousands of advertisements from commercials on TV and radio to displays in windows to classified ads in newspapers and magazines. We see billboards along roadsides and posters on signposts. All of this advertising has a single purpose: to persuade the audience to buy a particular product or service, or form an agreeable opinion about a specific issue. A careful review of advertising reveals that copywriters rely on special words that add power and appeal to their messages. In discussing the various advertising media with your students, be sure to emphasize the words of List 12.

ACTIVITY 1 — WORKSHEET 12–1, "BEING AN AD WRITER"

Objective:

Students are to select a favorite product and write an advertisement for it.

Procedure:

A few days in advance, you might ask your students to bring in examples of advertising copy from newspapers and magazines. Allow some time for the students to exchange the sample ads and discuss them. Emphasize how the ads are designed and written, particularly noting the use of advertising words.

Next, distribute copies of List 12 and briefly review the advertising words. You will likely find that many of these words appear in the ads your students have examined. Now hand out copies of Worksheet 12–1. Tell your students to think of a favorite product—a stereo, ten-speed bike, ski equipment, or even a comfortable sweater—complete the worksheet, and write an advertisement for this product. They should focus on its special features and why the reader would benefit from it.

ACTIVITY 2 — WRITE A CLASSIFIED AD

Objective:

Students are to write a classified advertisement.

Procedure:

Prior to this assignment you might collect some examples of classified advertisements in newspapers and magazines. You can also ask your students to bring in some examples. Provide time for sharing these examples of classifieds and emphasize that classifieds are a common and easy method of advertising items ranging from bicycles to cars to houses. Good classified ads emphasize the features of the items being sold. Just about anything can be sold through classifieds; there are even giveaways! For this assignment, your students are to imagine that they are selling something—their parents' house, a car, bicycle, stereo, or some other item—and they are to write a classified ad.

See List 13, Business Words; and List 14, Consumer Words.

List 12. Advertising Words

When companies advertise, they try to highlight the best features of their products or services. If you study advertisements carefully, you will see that many of the same words regularly appear in various ads. These words are known to have "pulling power" or audience appeal—they help sell the product or service.

best	health	proven
better	high (technology, fashion)	quality
brand new		reduce
choose	hurry	results
comfort	improved	safety
courteous	inexpensive	satisfaction
discovery	introducing	save
don't (wait, delay, miss)	love	service
	money	simple
easy	new	special
experience	now	successful
free	order (today, now)	take
fresh	perfect	unique
gift	prize	valuable
grand	professional	warranty
greatest	proof	well-known
guaranteed	protect	

NAME _____ DATE _____

BEING AN AD WRITER

DIRECTIONS: Complete this worksheet and write an advertisement for your favorite product.

1. What is the name of your product? _____

_____

2. What are at least three positive features of it? _____

_____

_____

3. What might a customer like about your product? _____

_____

_____

4. How would a customer benefit from the product? _____

_____

_____

5. What would be a catchy headline to start your advertisement? _____

_____

_____

13

BUSINESS WORDS

Teaching Suggestions

Every field of interest has its own vocabulary. Mastery of that vocabulary is a type of initiation into that field. The following list offers students a glimpse of the vocabulary used by people in business. Definitions are included, as many students may not be familiar with the meaning of some words.

ACTIVITY 1 — WORKSHEET 13–1, "STARTING YOUR OWN BUSINESS"

Objective:

Students are to write an imaginary account of starting a business.

Procedure:

After distributing List 13, discuss with your students what is necessary for the success of any business. You might talk about such factors as capital, overhead, a salable product or service, location, customers, advertising, fair price, and good service. Now ask your students to think about starting an enterprise of their own. Some examples include providing a grass-cutting service, babysitting, raising and selling vegetables, running errands for neighbors, and doing odd jobs. Hand out Worksheet 13–1 and point out that answering the questions on the worksheet will help them clarify their thoughts for the writing assignment.

ACTIVITY 2 — A PROFILE OF SUCCESS

Objective:

Students are to write a profile of what they consider to be a successful businessperson.

Procedure:

Instruct your students to think about what traits a businessperson must have if he or she is to be successful. Some things you might mention include ambition, drive, persistence, knowledge of a product or service, and a willingness to work long hours. For this assignment, students are to write a composition explaining the traits a successful businessperson is likely to have.

See List 12, Advertising Words; and List 14, Consumer Words.

List 13. Business Words

Following are words that successful businesspeople understand. If they don't, it's unlikely they'll stay in business very long!

advertising — a sales presentation directed to potential customers

asset — something of value owned by a company or a person

balance sheet — a periodic statement of a company's assets and liabilities

bankruptcy — the inability of a business or individual to meet financial obligations

capital — any property, assets, or money owned by an individual or business

cash flow — the inflow and outflow of cash

collateral — assets pledged to a lender to secure a loan; assets can be liquidated by the lender to recover the loan in case of a default

competition — rivalry among businesses for the same market

contract — a legal agreement between two or more parties

demand — the need or desire for specific goods or services

discount — a reduction in the price of a product or service

employee — a worker

employer — a person or business who provides work for people

entrepreneur — a person who finances and assumes the risk of new business ventures

inventory — the materials, supplies, and goods of a company

job — a position of employment

loan — an amount of money lent, usually to be repaid with interest

market strategy — a plan to achieve sales

need — the lack of something desired

objectives — goals of what a business seeks to accomplish

overhead — the typical operating expenses of a business

partnership — a legal agreement by which two or more people own and operate a business

price — the exchange value of a product or service

production — the conversion of materials into finished products

profit — what remains after the costs of production and marketing have been deducted from income

prospecting — the identification of potential customers

risk — taking a chance that is hoped to result in a gain but may result in a loss

salary — monetary compensation for employees

supply — to provide something that is needed; stock

NAME _____   DATE _____

STARTING YOUR OWN BUSINESS

DIRECTIONS: Think about the factors
responsible for the success of a business.
Providing a salable product or service,
obtaining capital, advertising, charging
a fair price, and providing good service
are certainly some considerations.
Think about starting a business of your
own. Answer the questions below and
write a composition about starting your
own business.

1. What business would you start? _____

2. What equipment, if any, would you need? _____

_____

3. Would you need capital to begin your business? If yes, how much and from whom would you

obtain it? _____

_____

_____

4. How would you let potential customers know about your business? _____

_____

5. What would your policy be toward dissatisfied customers? _____

_____

_____

14

CONSUMER WORDS

Teaching Suggestions

We are all consumers. An understanding of the words of this list will not only help students become more informed consumers, but will enable them to better comprehend the countless articles and books written for consumers each year.

ACTIVITY 1 — WORKSHEET 14–1, "BEING A SMART CONSUMER"

Objective:

Students are to think about buying something they really want, then write an essay describing how they would make sure that the product they buy meets their expectations.

Procedure:

Distribute copies of List 14 to your students and review the consumer words. Ask for volunteers to explain how they would go about buying something that is expensive. Do they comparison shop? Do they check prices, features, and warranties? What kinds of questions do they ask salespeople?

Now hand out copies of Worksheet 14–1. Ask your students to imagine that they are about to buy an expensive item they desire. How would they make sure that they were spending their money wisely? Students are to complete the worksheet and then write an essay describing how they would be a smart consumer.

ACTIVITY 2 — A LETTER TO THE COMPANY

Objective:

Students are to write a letter to a company about a product.

Procedure:

Ask your students to think of a product or service with which they are very satisfied or extremely disappointed. You might encourage volunteers to share some of their experiences. For this assignment, students are to write a letter to the company that made the product or provided the service, offering either praise, suggestions on how to improve it, or simply explaining why they are disappointed. Background Sheet 14 contains the block style and semiblock style for business letters. If students have the address of the company to which they are writing, they might mail their letters.

See List 12, Advertising Words; and List 13, Business Words.

LIST 14. CONSUMER WORDS

All of us are consumers. Because the audience is so big, numerous articles and books are written for consumers each year. You can be sure that many of the words of the following list also appear in those works.

arbitration	discount	product
bait-and-switch	estimate	quality
barter	features	rebate
budget	fraud	recall
buyer	free sample	refund
caveat emptor	generic	rent
chain letter	giveaway	return
comparison shop	guarantee	ripoff
con man (or woman)	installment	sale
contract	interest	sales letter
credit	investment	salesperson
credit card	labeling	sales receipt
credit rating	layaway	service
customer	lease	service contract
debt	liability	trade
deed	merchandise	trade-in
depreciation	price	warranty

NAME _____ DATE _____

BEING A SMART CONSUMER

DIRECTIONS: Think about an expensive product that you really would like. It may be a stereo system, a ten-speed bike, a computer system, a TV, new furniture for your room, maybe something even better. What would you do to make sure the product you buy is the best value and meets your expectations? First answer the questions below, then write an essay about how you would be a smart consumer.

1. What product would you buy? _____

   _____

2. Why do you want this? _____

   _____

3. Would you comparison shop? Why or why not? _____

   _____

   _____

4. What questions would you ask the salesperson about your product? _____

   _____

   _____

   _____

5. How could you be sure that the product you buy is the best value for your money? ____

   _____

   _____

   _____

Background Sheet 14. Sample Business-Letter Forms

BLOCK STYLE

Your Name
Your Street
Your City, State, Zip
Date

Name and Title of Addressee
Company Name
Street
City, State, Zip

Dear Mr./Ms. (Name of Person):

Paragraphs are *not* indented in the body.

Sincerely,

Your Name

SEMIBLOCK STYLE

                                        Your Name
                                        Your Street
                                        Your City, State, Zip
                                        Date

Name and Title of Addressee
Company Name
Street
City, State, Zip

Dear Mr./Ms. (Name of Person):

   Paragraphs *are* indented in the body.

                                        Sincerely,

                                        Your Name

15

CRAFT WORDS

Teaching Suggestions

Working with crafts offers enjoyment, relaxation, and an outlet for creativity. Most people experience much satisfaction and pride in producing an item with their own hands. It is likely that many of your students enjoy some type of craft.

ACTIVITY 1 — WORKSHEET 15–1, "I MADE IT"

Objective:

Students are to write a description of something they created or built.

Procedure:

Hand out copies of List 15 and review the various crafts with your students. Ask if any of them work with crafts. It is likely that many do. You might ask some of these students to share their experiences with the class.

Next, distribute copies of Worksheet 15–1. Ask your students if they have ever built something. It might have been a craft item, a treehouse, a snow fort, a model, a puppet, a volcano for a science project—at one time or another they have all made something. Instruct them to write an article about their creation. Answering the questions on the worksheet first will help them organize their thoughts.

ACTIVITY 2 — THE HOW AND WHY OF DOING A CRAFT

Objective:

Students are to write about a craft they enjoy, how they do the craft, and why they enjoy it.

Procedure:

Ask your students if they do crafts. It is likely that many do. Ask for volunteers to share with the class any crafts they enjoy and discuss with them why people enjoy crafts. For the assignment, students are to write an article describing a craft they enjoy. They should include any special skills or materials that are necessary as well as why they enjoy this activity.

See List 21, Hobby Words; and List 23, Sports Words.

LIST 15. CRAFT WORDS

Crafts offer people a chance to produce something with their own hands, through their own efforts. For many people, crafts are an enjoyable pastime. Others sell their handiwork and turn their skills into a successful business. In either case, few things are as satisfying as those we create ourselves.

basketry	jewelry making	printmaking
batik	knitting	quilting
calligraphy	lace making	rug hooking
candlemaking	leather working	sculpture
carpentry	macramé	sewing
ceramics	metal working	stained glass
crocheting	model building	stenciling
doll making	needlepoint	stone carving
egg decorating	painting	tie-dyeing
embroidery	papercrafts	toy making
enameling	paper-mâché	weaving
fabric painting	pottery	woodworking

NAME _____   DATE _____

I MADE IT

DIRECTIONS: Think of something you have made. It might be a craft item, or something else. Answer the questions below and then write an article about what you made.

1. What did you make? _____

   _____

2. What was it for? _____

   _____

3. What materials did you use? _____

   _____

   _____

4. What special skills and tools did you use? _____

   _____

   _____

   _____

5. What steps did you take in producing your creation? _____

   _____

   _____

   _____

6. What eventually happened to your creation? _____

   _____

   _____

16

ECOLOGY WORDS

Teaching Suggestions

As we become more aware of the dynamic relationships of the organisms of our world to each other, as well as to their environment, we realize how complex the webs of life are. The following list by no means includes all the words and concepts of ecology, but it does contain the basics and provides a good starting point. Emphasize to your students that these words are used by authors who write about nature and its wondrous diversity.

ACTIVITY 1 — WORKSHEET 16–1, "A SPEECH ABOUT THE ENVIRONMENT"

Objective:

Students are to select a topic about ecology, and write and give a speech about it.

Procedure:

Hand out copies of List 16 and review it with your students. Point out that ecology is the study of the interactions and relationships between organisms and their environment. For this assignment, instruct your students to pick a topic from the words of List 16, or choose any other topic of their own regarding ecology. They are to research their topics, write a speech, and give their speech to the class.

Now distribute copies of Worksheet 16–1. Explain to your students that completing the worksheet will help them organize their speech. You should encourage them to use the library to develop their material with pertinent facts and details. Be sure to allow enough time at the end of the assignment for students to give their speeches to the class.

ACTIVITY 2 — CHANGING PLACES

Objective:

Students are to imagine that they are a plant or animal that lives in their home or yard; they are to describe their environment from this viewpoint.

Procedure:

Ask your students to pretend that they are a plant or animal that lives in their yard or home. If they were this plant or animal, how would they see their environment? For example, to a squirrel, a tree appears to be much larger than it does to us; yet a squirrel is entirely at ease in that tree. We might consider the tree to be little more than a decoration for the yard, but to the squirrel it provides safety and a home. Emphasize that when we change viewpoints, we also change perceptions. For the assignment, students are to put themselves in the place of a plant or animal and write a composition describing their environment from this viewpoint.

LIST 16. ECOLOGY WORDS

Ecology—the study of living things and their relationships to each other and the environment—is as broad as the world itself. The following list focuses on some of the most important words and concepts in ecology.

acid rain	fish	pollution
adaptation	flora	pond
animals	food web	population
bacteria	forest	prairie
balance of nature	grassland	precipitation
biomes	greenhouse effect	predator
birds	habitat	prey
bog	host	producer
carnivore	humus	rain forest
climate	inorganic	reptiles
community	insects	respiration
competition	instinct	rivers
conservation	interaction	savanna
consumer	invertebrates	scavenger
cycle	lake	soil
decay	mammals	species
decomposers	microorganisms	streams
decomposition	mountain	succession
desert	natural resources	symbiosis
ecosystem	natural selection	taiga
endangered species	nutrients	territoriality
energy	oceans	trees
erosion	omnivore	tropic
environment	organic	tundra
estuary	oxygen	vegetation
evaporation	parasite	vertebrates
evolution	peat	watershed
extinct	photosynthesis	weather
fauna	plants	wetlands

NAME _____   DATE _____

A SPEECH ABOUT THE ENVIRONMENT

DIRECTIONS: Select a topic in ecology. Answer the following questions and then write a speech about your topic. Give your speech to the class.

1. What is your topic? _____
_____

2. Why did you choose this topic? _____
_____
_____

3. Why should people be aware of your topic? _____
_____
_____
_____

4. Can understanding of your topic help improve the environment? If yes, how? If no, why not?
_____
_____
_____

5. Does your topic have significance for the future? If yes, in what way? _____
_____
_____

17

EDUCATION WORDS

Teaching Suggestions

Most students find it easier to write about topics with which they have direct experience. School surely is one such topic. The words of this list will provide students with the vocabulary needed to write about school-related topics and issues.

ACTIVITY 1 — WORKSHEET 17–1, "WHAT'S RIGHT AND WRONG WITH MY SCHOOL"

Objective:

Students are to write a composition describing what they feel is right and wrong with their school.

Procedure:

Hand out List 17 and briefly review it with your students. Generate a discussion about your school, encouraging the students to share their feelings about its good points as well as areas in which they feel it can be improved. Tell them that their assignment is to write a composition about the positive and negative features of their school. Next, distribute Worksheet 17–1 and explain that they are to list their ideas on the worksheet before writing. After the activity, you might display the compositions, as students will be interested in the opinions of their classmates.

Extension:

Divide your students into groups of two or three. Suggest that they design and make a report card in which they grade their school. Encourage them to use construction paper or oak tag for their report cards.

ACTIVITY 2 — IF I WERE A TEACHER

Objective:

Students are to imagine that they are teachers and write a composition about the changes that they would make in conducting the class.

Procedure:

Distribute List 17 and review the words. Begin the activity by explaining to students that every teacher has different instructional methods—this is because teachers are individuals. Now ask them to think about the methods their teachers use that they, as students, like best. Some students may prefer independent study, others may like to listen to lectures, still others may prefer learning by way of discussion. Ask your students to imagine that they are teachers. What subject would they teach? How would they set up and conduct the class? What rules would they demand be followed? Instruct them to write a composition of how they would conduct class if they were the teacher.

See List 19, Words of Government and Politics.

List 17. Education Words

Not too long ago, Americans attended class in one-room schoolhouses. Today, it is not uncommon for a student to go to preschool, elementary school, middle school, high school, college, and graduate school. Following are words that have become a part of the American educational establishment.

achievement	grade	problem solving
activity	graduation	professor
administrator	group	program
assessment	guidance counselor	promotion
assignment	high school	pupil
basics	higher education	question
behavior	homework	reading
book	honor roll	remediation
children	illiteracy	research
class	instruction	responsibility
classroom	instructor	resources
college	IQ (intelligence	retention
communication	quotient)	schedule
content	knowledge	school
course	learning	score
creativity	lesson	sports
curriculum	library	student
degree	literacy	study
dialogue	mastery	subject matter
diploma	mathematics	teacher
discipline	mentor	test
dropout	middle school	text
elementary school	motivation	theory
evaluation	objective	thinking
example	pass	university
fail	peer	vocational
feedback	percentage	writing
goal		

NAME _____   DATE _____

WHAT'S RIGHT AND WRONG WITH MY SCHOOL

DIRECTIONS: Everything in life has good points and bad. School is no exception. Fill out this worksheet and write an essay entitled "What's Right and Wrong with My School."

1. List at least three things that are "right" with your school: _____

_____

_____

_____

_____

_____

2. List at least three things that are "wrong" with your school: _____

_____

_____

_____

_____

_____

3. How can the wrongs be improved? _____

_____

_____

_____

_____

18

FOOD WORDS

Teaching Suggestions

Countless articles and books about food are written each year. These works range from the latest recipes for exotic delicacies to articles warning about pesticide residue on our vegetables. The following list provides the basics that will help your students write about food effectively.

ACTIVITY 1 — WORKSHEET 18–1, "IT'S TIME TO FEAST"

Objective:

Students are to write a descriptive composition about a feast of their favorite foods.

Procedure:

Begin the activity by distributing List 18. Briefly review the words with the students. Next, ask volunteers to describe their favorite foods. For the assignment, students are to imagine they are having a feast—a full course dinner—of their favorite foods and write a descriptive composition about it. Filling in Worksheet 18–1 will help students organize and develop their compositions.

ACTIVITY 1 — MAKE A MEAL PLAN

Objective:

Students are to design a week-long meal plan; they are to write a descriptive paragraph of their meal plans.

Procedure:

Distribute List 18 and review it with your students. Encourage a discussion of the importance of good nutrition and a balanced diet. You might ask your students to mention examples of healthy foods and junk foods. You might also briefly discuss the four basic food groups: the bread and cereal group, fruit and vegetable group, meat group (including fish, poultry, and eggs), and the dairy group (which includes anything made from milk).

For the activity, explain that students are to design a one-week meal plan. They are to include breakfast, lunch, and dinner, as well as snacks. An effective way to complete this part of the assignment is to develop the meal plan in the form of a chart. Students will find much of the information they will need from List 18; however, they should be allowed to use resource books if they wish. It may be advisable to work on this activity over a few periods.

After students have completed their charts, they are to write a paragraph summarizing their meal plans. On completion of the activity, you may wish to display the charts and paragraphs.

List 18. Food Words

Eating is often described as one of the great joys in life. Whereas our ancient ancestors were limited to nuts, roots, wild vegetables, and coarse meat, we can pick from a variety of dishes that entice our taste buds. Many authors earn their bread by writing about food.

additive	chef	fiber
appetite	cholesterol	fish
appetizer	chow	flour
bagel	condiments	fork
bake	cook	French fires
biscuit	cookie	fruit
boil	cottage cheese	fry
bread	crackers	goulash
breakfast	cuisine	gourmet
broil	culinary	grain
brunch	cutlery	gravy
butter	dessert	herb
cake	diet	honey
calorie	digestion	ice cream
candy	dinner	junk food
carbohydrate	dish	ketchup
cellulose	egg	kitchen
cheese	fat	knife

kosher	peanut	shellfish
leftovers	pepper	snack
lunch	pickles	soup
margarine	pie	spaghetti
mayonnaise	poach	spoon
meat	popcorn	stew
meatball	poultry	stuffing
milk	preservative	sugar
minerals	protein	toast
mustard	pudding	TV dinner
napkins	recipe	vegetable
nuts	salad	venison
omelet	salt	vitamin
pancake	sandwich	water
pasta	sauce	yogurt
pastry	seeds	

NAME _____   DATE _____

IT'S TIME TO FEAST

DIRECTIONS: Think of your favorite
foods. If you could plan your favorite
meal, what would you have? Complete
this worksheet and then write a composition about your favorite foods in the
best meal of your life.

Appetizers: _____

_____

Soups: _____

_____

Main Course: _____

_____

_____

Desserts: _____

_____

Beverages: _____

_____

With whom would you share your feast? Why? _____

_____

_____

19

WORDS OF GOVERNMENT AND POLITICS

Teaching Suggestions

While politicians love to spin catchy phrases to explain their latest proposals, government agencies regularly invent new words and terminology to describe their programs and policies. There never seems to be a shortage of governmental or political gobbledygook. The words of the following list will *not* be found on any one government document or in any one political platform, but they constitute a basic vocabulary for anyone who wants to write about the American political scene.

ACTIVITY 1 — WORKSHEET 19–1, "PERSONAL POLICIES"

Objective:

Students are to write a composition of change they would make in their town if they were mayor.

Procedure:

Hand out List 19 and review it with your students. Mention briefly the role that government and politics plays in a democratic society. Next, hand out Worksheet 19–1. Instruct your students to assume that they are the mayor of their town and that they have the power to change the way the town is run. What changes would they make? Why? Students are to first complete the worksheet and then write a composition describing the changes they would make in their town.

ACTIVITY 2 — A STUDENT BILL OF RIGHTS

Objective:

Students are to write a Student Bill of Rights.

Procedure:

Discuss the Bill of Rights with your students. (You might wish to work with their history teacher on this one.) Ask them to consider what rights students should have, then instruct them to write a Student Bill of Rights. As an added incentive, you can permit students to work in small groups for this activity. At the end of the assignment, you might combine the best features of the compositions and make a class Student Bill of Rights.

Extension:

Carry this activity a step further and have the groups write a School Constitution that outlines the roles of administrators, teachers, and students in their school. It would be helpful to briefly review the U.S. Constitution first for this activity.

See List 17, Education Words.

List 19. Words of Government and Politics

Government employees and politicians are two of the greatest inventors of words and phrases. New ideas, changes in policies, and fresh regulations require explanations and directions. The following list contains important words relating to government and politics.

accountability
administration
agency
alien
alliance
amendments
appointee
arms control
assistance
authorize
ballot
benefits
Bill of Rights
budget
bureaucracy
cabinet
campaign
caucus
centralization
citizen
city
civil rights
civil service
committee
compromise
Congress
Congressman/woman
conservative
Constitution
convention
coordination
corruption
council
county
court
decision making
Declaration of
    Independence

delegate
Democrat
document
efficiency
election
ethics
evaluation
executive
federal
filibuster
foreign policy
goals
grants
House of
    Representatives
income tax
institution
integrity
interest groups
international
judiciary
jury
law
leadership
Left (the)
legislation
legislature
liberal
lobby
management
mayor
media advisor
mediation
Medicare
nation
objectives
ombudsman
organization

patriotism
patronage
petition
pluralism
policy
political action
    committees
    (PACs)
political parties
poll
pragmatism
president
primary
program
propaganda
public
public opinion
quotas
reactionary
red tape
referendum
Republican
revolution
Right (the)
rights
Senate
Senator
sound bite
staff
state
Supreme Court
survey
tax
town
union
United Nations
veto
vote

NAME _____   DATE _____

PERSONAL POLICIES

DIRECTIONS: Imagine that you have just been appointed mayor of your town. You have the authority to change the way the town is run. What changes would you make, if any? Complete this worksheet and write a composition about the changes you would make in your town. Be sure to include valid reasons.

1. How did you become mayor? _____

_____

2. What if any special qualifications do you have? _____

_____

_____

3. What policy, rule, or law would you change first? Why? _____

_____

_____

_____

4. What other policies, rules, or laws would you change? Why? _____

_____

_____

5. How would these changes improve your town? _____

_____

_____

20

HEALTH WORDS

Teaching Suggestions

Health is a topic that is often ignored by students. After all, most teenagers feel invincible. As our population ages and many people become health conscious, the words of the following list increase in significance. Many of these words can be found in the countless health articles and books that are published each year.

ACTIVITY 1 — WORKSHEET 20–1, "A SUBJECT OF HEALTH"

Objective:

Students are to write an article on a health topic.

Procedure:

Distribute copies of List 20 to your students. Briefly review it, then ask them to volunteer what they feel are significant health problems. Suggestions might include AIDS, cancer, heart disease, drug abuse, alcoholism, smoking, lack of proper nutrition, and insufficient exercise. You might list these topics on the board.

For the assignment, students are to select one of the health topics and write an article about it. Students will need to do research for this assignment, and Worksheet 20–1 will help them focus their research. You might wish to arrange for library time. For current topics, suggest that students check *The Readers' Guide to Periodical Literature*, which will help them find appropriate magazine articles for their research.

ACTIVITY 2 — HOW TO GET ALONG WITH PEOPLE

Objective:

Students are to write an essay on how to get along with others.

Procedure:

Briefly discuss with your students that good physical health is closely linked to emotional health. One of the aspects of emotional health is having good personal relationships with others. The development of positive relationships depends on the ability to get along with other people. For this assignment, students are to write an essay entitled "How to Get Along with People."

To help students clarify their thoughts, suggest that they compose a simple listing of ideas. On one side of a sheet of paper they should list four or five behaviors that they like in some of the people they know. On the other side of the sheet, they should list four or five behaviors that they don't like. From this they should be able to develop their essays. Remind them to include specific details and examples.

List 20. Health Words

Good health is truly a blessing, yet most of us fail to appreciate its value until it is lost. Following are words associated with health.

accident	diabetes	medicine
aging	dialysis	metabolism
AIDS	diet	nausea
alcoholism	digestion	nutrition
allergies	disability	obesity
anemia	disease	organ transplants
antibiotic	disorder	pain killers
antihistamine	drug abuse	penicillin
anxiety	epidemic	pharmacy
appendicitis	exercise	phobia
arthritis	fatigue	pneumonia
aspirin	first aid	poisoning
attitude	flu	respiration
backache	headache	seizures
bacteria	heart disease	senility
biofeedback	heredity	sleep
biopsy	hyperactivity	smoking
bronchitis	hypertension	stress
cancer	hypothermia	stroke
checkup	immune system	substance abuse
cholesterol	immunization	surgery
circulation	infection	vaccination
colds	insomnia	virus
coma	insulin	ulcers
cough	kidney disease	weight
deafness	leukemia	X-rays
depression		

NAME _____ DATE _____

A SUBJECT OF HEALTH

DIRECTIONS: Select a topic in health and write an article about it. Completing this worksheet first will help you focus your research efforts.

1. What health topic have you selected to write about? _____

_____

2. Why is this topic important to you? _____

_____

_____

3. Write at least three questions about your topic that you hope to answer during the course of

your research: _____

_____

_____

_____

_____

_____

_____

_____

_____

21

HOBBY WORDS

Teaching Suggestions

Everyone needs a hobby, and most people have at least one. It is likely that several different hobbies are enjoyed by the students in your class.

ACTIVITY 1 — WORKSHEET 21–1, "MY HOBBY"

Objective:

Students are to write a composition about their hobbies.

Procedure:

Distribute copies of List 21 and review it with your students. Conduct a discussion about hobbies. To begin the assignment, hand out Worksheet 21–1 and explain that students are to complete the worksheet and then write a composition about their hobbies. They should include why they like this hobby and what it entails.

ACTIVITY 2 — AFTER-SCHOOL ACTIVITIES

Objective:

Students are to write an essay entitled "Why Our School Should (or Should Not) Run After-School Hobbies."

Procedure:

Many schools run after-school activities or hobbies for their students. If your school does, instruct your students to write an essay on why they feel this program is or is not worthwhile. Encourage them to support their ideas with details and examples. If your school does not have an activities program or if your students would prefer activities that are not offered, they should write their essays explaining their feelings on these angles.

Extension:

If your school doesn't have an activities program and the students are in favor of one, you might pass the compositions along to the appropriate administrators to see if a program can be established. This would provide students with a strong incentive to develop their ideas and write clearly.

See List 15, Craft Words; and List 23, Sports Words.

List 21. Hobby Words

Hobbies offer people a chance for fun, relaxation, and a feeling of accomplishment. They can be a pleasant escape from the rigors and stresses of the modern world. Following is a list of popular hobbies.

antique collecting	flower arranging	reading
arts and crafts	flower collecting	rock collecting
baking	gardening	scrapbooks
bird watching	hiking	seashell collecting
boating	magic	sewing
book collecting	miniatures	singing
butterfly collecting	music	sketching
camping	nature study	sports
card collecting	painting	stamp collecting
chess	pets	stenciling
coin collecting	photography	travel
cooking	puppetry	volunteering
dancing	puzzles	working on cars
dramatics	radio-controlled vehicles	writing
doll collecting		
fishing		

NAME _____   DATE _____

MY HOBBY

DIRECTIONS: Think about your hobbies. Select one, complete this worksheet, and then write a composition about your hobby.

1. My hobby is: _____

2. How does one participate in your hobby? _____

_____

_____

_____

3. Why do you like this hobby? _____

_____

_____

_____

4. Describe any special materials necessary for your hobby. _____

_____

_____

_____

5. To whom would you recommend your hobby? Why? _____

_____

_____

22

WORDS OF NEWSPAPERS AND MAGAZINES

Teaching Suggestions

Newspapers and magazines offer a variety of features and articles. They are significant sources of information. While some publications are designed for a specific audience, others remain general in appeal.

Most newspaper and general magazine articles are written using short, clear sentences. Articles may rely on research and interviews or may be based on observation or firsthand experience.

Virtually all magazine articles adhere to a simple structure consisting of an opening, body, and conclusion. A good opening introduces the topic, grabs the reader's attention, and leads into the body. The body should focus on the *five Ws* plus *how*:

- What happened?
- When did it happen?
- Who was involved?
- Where did it happen?
- Why did it happen?
- *H*ow did it happen?

The conclusion should be brief and contain a final point or idea for the reader.

While some articles in newspapers follow this same structure, straight news does not. In straight news, all or some of the *five Ws* and *how* are usually covered in the lead which is the opening of the article. The rest of the article supplies additional details, arranged from most important to least important. A conclusion is generally not used.

ACTIVITY 1 — WORKSHEET 22–1, "GET THE SCOOP!"

Objective:

Students are to select an event, observe it, and write a newspaper article about it.

Procedure:

A few days before this activity, ask your students to bring in copies of newspapers. After distributing and reviewing List 22 and its sublist, hand out the newspapers. Allow students to work in small groups while examining the newspapers. Ask for volunteers to identify some of the different parts.

Next, hand out Worksheet 22–1. Explain that students are to select an event—perhaps a school sporting event, a dance, the ride home on the bus, lunch at the school cafeteria, an assembly—pretend they are reporters, observe the event, and write an article about it. Discuss the *five Ws* and *how* and encourage them to use the worksheet to help them organize their articles. Also encourage them to interview participants in the event. Background Sheet 22 can help students conduct effective interviews. On completion of the activity, you might wish to publish the articles in a class newspaper.

ACTIVITY 2 — WRITE AN EDITORIAL

Objective:

Students are to select a meaningful topic and write an editorial.

Procedure:

Explain the difference between an editorial and a news article. Essentially, while an article is written to impart facts or information, the purpose of an editorial is to persuade the reader to accept the author's viewpoints on an issue or topic.

Ask your students to volunteer some issues that concern them. A few examples might include: strict parents, being misunderstood, too much homework; censorship; local, national, or international issues. List their ideas on the board. Instruct them to select an issue and write an editorial in which they try to convince their readers to accept their position. Encourage them to structure their editorials with an opening in which their issue is introduced, a body in which it is explained, and a closing in which they make a recommendation or call for action.

List 22. Words of Newspapers and Magazines

People read newspapers and magazines for information and entertainment. Because their readerships are usually diverse, most newspapers and magazines publish a variety of material. Even when a publication is slanted to a particular audience or subject, it may still carry many kinds of articles, features, and columns. Following are words associated with newspapers and magazines.

accuracy	edition	lead para-	scoop
advertising	editor	graph	sidebar
anecdotes	editorial	lead story	slant
angle	editor-in-chief	libel laws	source
AP (Associat-	entertainment	managing	staff
ed Press)	facts	editor	straight news
audience	feature story	news story	stringer
balance	filler	nonfiction	style
breaking	First Amend-	obituary	subject
story	ment	opinion	supplement
bureau	foreign corre-	photo essay	syndicated
byline	spondent	photographs	feature
cartoons	freelance	press confer-	tabloid
circulation	headline	ence	tip
city desk	human	press release	UPI (United
column	interest	publisher	Press In-
copy editor	information	query	ternation-
cover story	investigative	quote	al)
dateline	reporter	readership	wire service
deadline		reporter	wire story

Sublist — **Types of Articles Found in Newspapers and Magazines**

book/movie/	features	informational	opinion
theater	food	inspirational	pets
reviews	gardening	interview	politics
business	general interest	investigative	profile
crafts	historical	reporting	psychology
editorials	home repair	local news	real estate
essays	how-to	medical	science
exposé	human interest	obituary	sports
fashion	humor		

NAME _____   DATE _____

GET THE SCOOP!

DIRECTIONS: Select a newsworthy event at school—perhaps a dance, football game, assembly, or special discussion. Imagine that you are a reporter. Attend the event, take notes, interview participants if possible, and write an article about it. Build your article around the *five Ws* and *how* by answering the following questions.

1. What was the event? _____

_____

2. Where did the event take place? _____

_____

3. Who was involved? _____

_____

4. When did it happen? _____

_____

5. Why did it happen? _____

_____

6. How did the event happen? _____

_____

7. What was the result? _____

_____

Background Sheet 22. Tips for Effective Interviews

- For your interview, select someone who knows about your topic.

- Gather background information on your topic and develop a list of questions for the interview.

- Avoid using questions that can be answered by a simple yes or no; instead, ask questions that require explanations. Follow up interesting (or confusing) answers with additional questions.

- During the interview, listen carefully and write down important notes. (Avoid trying to write down everything the person says—you won't be able to and you'll end up missing essential facts.)

- If you are unsure of something, ask for clarification.

- If you want to quote someone, be sure to use the person's exact words.

- At the end of the interview, review important information with the interviewee.

- Always thank the person you interviewed for his or her time and help.

23

SPORTS WORDS

Teaching Suggestions

Most people participate in sports for the challenge of competition, for enjoyment, or for relaxation. It is likely that many of your students enjoy one or more sports. This enjoyment can be a wellspring for writing ideas.

ACTIVITY 1 — WORKSHEET 23–1, "THE RULES AND STRATEGIES OF THE GAME"

Objective:

Students are to select a favorite sport and write a descriptive account of it.

Procedure:

Distribute copies of List 23 to your students and review the sports. Ask for volunteers to briefly describe the sports they enjoy. For the activity, hand out Worksheet 23–1. Instruct your students to select one of their favorite sports and write a description of how they participate in it. They should include an explanation of its rules and strategies. Answering the questions on the worksheet will help students focus their ideas before writing.

ACTIVITY 2 — BE A SPORTSWRITER

Objective:

Students are to attend a school sporting event and write an article about it.

Procedure:

A few days in advance of this activity, you might wish to ask students to bring in the sports sections of various newspapers. Allow some time for them to examine the articles. Point out some of the features—articles have headlines, are usually written in short sentences, may include interviews or quotes from some of the people involved, and will contain the scores and other facts about the event. Instruct your students to attend a school sporting event of their choice and write an article about it. Encourage them to take notes during the event so that they will have all the important facts and details.

See List 15, Craft Words; and List 21, Hobby Words.

List 23. Sports Words

The thrill of competition stirs most of us. Sports offer the opportunity to test our athletic powers as well as have fun. Following are words that are related to sports. Many of them will be familiar.

archery	competition	hunting
athlete	conditioning	ice hockey
auto racing	equipment	ice sailing
badminton	exercise	ice skating
ballooning	fans	judge
baseball	fencing	judo
basketball	field hockey	karate
bicycling	fishing	kayaking
billiards	football	lacrosse
boat racing	game	loser
body building	golf	marathon races
bowling	gymnastics	match
boxing	handball	motorcycle racing
bullfighting	hang gliding	mountain climbing
canoeing	harness racing	official
championship	horseback riding	opponent
coach	horse racing	playoff
commentators	horseshoes	practice

racquetball	snowmobiling	track and field
rafting	soccer	training
referee	softball	trophy
rowing	spectators	umpire
rugby	speedboating	volleyball
rules	squash	water-skiing
running	surfing	weight lifting
sailing	swimming	winner
scuba diving	team	wrestling
skiing	tennis	yachting
sky diving		

NAME _____   DATE _____

THE RULES AND STRATEGIES OF THE GAME

DIRECTIONS: Think of the sport that you enjoy most either as a participant or a spectator. Answer the questions on the worksheet and then write a composition describing the rules of your sport and how it is played.

1. What sport did you choose? _____

2. Why do you enjoy this sport? _____

_____

_____

_____

3. Are you a participant, spectator, or both? Explain: _____

_____

_____

4. What are the rules of this sport? _____

_____

_____

_____

_____

5. What are the basic strategies? _____

_____

_____

_____

_____

24

TRAVEL WORDS

Teaching Suggestions

We are a mobile people. We like to travel. With modern transportation we can travel long distances quickly and at a reasonable cost. Wherever one goes—whether on a business trip, vacation, or simply sightseeing on a Sunday afternoon—knowing the following words will be helpful.

ACTIVITY 1 — WORKSHEET 24–1, "TRAVELING AROUND"

Objective:

Students are to write an account of a trip they recently took.

Procedure:

Hand out copies of List 24 and review it. Many of the words will be familiar, but you should explain any that aren't. Next, distribute Worksheet 24–1. Instruct your students to think of a trip they took—it might have been a vacation, or merely a daytrip to visit a relative. They are to complete the worksheet, which will help them clarify and organize their thoughts, and then write a composition about the trip.

ACTIVITY 2 — AN IMAGINARY TRIP

Objective:

Students are to write an account of an imaginary trip.

Procedure:

Ask your students to think of a place they would like to visit. It can be anywhere—a distant city or even the moon. Why do they want to go there? What would they take? Who would they take if they could invite anyone they wished? What things would they take? What would they expect to see? How would they get there, and how would they return? They should then write a descriptive composition about their trip.

List 24. Travel Words

With modern transportation, people are traveling to distant places more than ever. Understanding the following travel words can make most trips easier and more enjoyable.

abroad	fare	rent
accommodations	first class	reservations
adventure	gratuity	resort
airline	hotel	round trip
airplane	immunization	ship
airport	inn	sightseeing
bed and breakfast	itinerary	ticket
bellboy	luggage	time sharing
booking	meal plan	time zone
bumping	motel	tour
bus	motor lodge	tourist
cancellation	off-season	train
car	overseas	transfers
charter	package tour	travel agent
credit cards	passport	travel brochure
cruise	plans	traveler's checks
currency	rates	trip
customs	recreation	vacation
destination	relaxation	visa
entertainment		

NAME _____   DATE _____

TRAVELING AROUND

DIRECTIONS: Think of a trip you recently took. It might be a trip with your parents or friends, a class trip, or one you took alone. Complete this worksheet and write a composition about your trip.

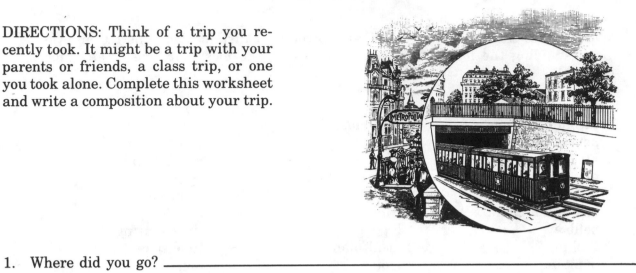

1. Where did you go? _____

2. When did you go? _____

3. Who went with you? _____

   _____

4. What did you take along? _____

   _____

   _____

5. Describe some of the things you saw or visited: _____

   _____

   _____

   _____

6. What was the most memorable event of your trip? _____

   _____

   _____

section lll

Lists and Activities for Fiction Writing

25

WORDS OF ADVENTURE AND ROMANCE

Teaching Suggestions

We all like stories of adventure and romance. Because of their popularity with students, adventure and romance provide a good field for writing activities.

ACTIVITY 1 — WORKSHEET 25–1, "THE CONTINUING ADVENTURES OF . . ."

Objective:

Students are to select a favorite character from an adventure or romance story and write a new story for that character.

Procedure:

Distribute copies of List 25 and review the words with your students. Explain that all these words may be found in stories of adventure or romance. Ask your students to name some examples of these kinds of stories. Encourage them to name books as well as movies. Note that many stories are a combination of adventure and romance and that most rely on fast action and interesting characters. The good stories are exciting and absorbing, and the reader or viewer usually winds up rooting for the good guys.

For the assignment, students are to complete Worksheet 25–1 first and then write their stories.

Extension:

Ask your students to create a new hero or heroine, and write an adventure or romance story.

ACTIVITY 2 — THE COMPLETE CHARACTER

Objective:

Students are to select a character from a favorite adventure or romance story and write a descriptive composition about that character.

Procedure:

Hand out copies of List 25 and review it with your students. Explain that the lead characters of adventure and romance stories are handsome or beautiful and possess compelling magnetism. They are designed to capture the interest of the audience or reader. Moreover, they almost always find themselves in exotic settings and seemingly hopeless situations. The story's appeal is centered around the characters—readers or viewers want to find out what happens to the character next.

For this assignment, students are to select a favorite character from an adventure or romance story and write a descriptive composition of that character. Encourage them to briefly summarize the story from which they took the character, describe the character physically and emotionally, and then tell what they feel is the character's most appealing point.

See List 29, Words of Science Fiction and Fantasy; List 30, Spy, Detective, and Mystery Words; and List 31, Western Words.

List 25. Words of Adventure and Romance

Cliffhangers, chase scenes, impossible escapes, excitement, and love are the ingredients of adventure and romance stories. They usually have clear-cut heroes, heroines, and villains, making it easy to root for the good guys and gals. These stories make up a large part of the published fiction every year. They can be as fun to write as they are to read. The following list contains words you will find in stories of adventure and romance.

abduct	forbidden	lover's	seek
agent	forgiven	triangle	shrewd
anxiety	girlfriend	lusty	sigh
apprehension	goodbye	marry	smile
arouse	good-looking	melancholy	sneaky
beautiful	grief	miss	snuggle
betray	grin	mourn	soft
boyfriend	handsome	need	startle
breakup	happy	nervous	steal
broken heart	heartbreak	obstacle	stubborn
brutality	heartless	passion	suicide
chase	hero	peril	sympathy
confidence	heroine	pine	tears
confusion	hostage	plan	tease
crafty	hug	possess	tender
cruel	humorous	pout	thwart
cry	ignore	protect	timid
danger	interest	ransom	torture
defensive	jilt	rapture	tragic
depression	joy	reconcile	trap
desire	kidnap	regret	trick
despair	kill	remorse	trust
divorce	kiss	rescue	tryst
double-cross	leave	resent	two-timer
ecstasy	let down	revenge	villain
embrace	lie	ruin	uncertain
emotion	lips	save	want
evil	lose	scheme	warm
feeling	love	scorn	warn
find	lovely	search	waver
flirt	lover	security	wicked
foolish			

NAME _____ DATE _____

THE CONTINUING ADVENTURES OF . . .

DIRECTIONS: Think of a favorite character from an adventure or love story. You may have read the story in a book or seen it in the movies or on TV. After completing this worksheet, write a new story for your character.

1. Who is your character? _____

2. Why did you choose this character? _____

_____

3. Describe your character's emotional traits: _____

_____

_____

_____

4. Describe your character's physical traits: _____

_____

_____

_____

5. On the back of this sheet, briefly list ideas about the story you will write.

26

WORDS OF FOLKLORE

Teaching Suggestions

The word *folklore* is like an umbrella. It covers several types of narrative prose found throughout the oral traditions of the world. While folklore includes myths, legends, fairy tales, tall tales, fables, and songs, this list is limited to American folk tales. Generally, folklore is highly creative and often interweaves truth and imagination. Folklore may pass in and out of written literature and may contain morals or lessons. The stories invariably offer a unique insight into the people who invented them. When teaching folklore, try reading some out loud to your students. Modeling can be an effective teaching technique and can help your activity get off to a strong start.

ACTIVITY 1 — WORKSHEET 26–1, "INVENTING A FOLK TALE"

Objective:

Students are to write a modern folk tale.

Procedure:

Distribute copies of List 26 and review the words with your students. Briefly discuss the scope of folklore and go over the included sublist. It is likely that most students will be familiar with some of the stories. (You might wish to obtain an anthology of folk tales from your library and keep it in the classroom for reference.) Explain that many of the American folk stories focused on characters who had specific occupations. Paul Bunyan was a lumberjack, John Henry was a railroad man, and Annie Oakley was a sharpshooting showwoman.

To begin this assignment, hand out Worksheet 26–1. Instruct your students to select a modern occupation and write a modern folk tale about it, using the worksheet to organize their ideas. At the end of the activity, you may consider compiling a class folk tale book.

ACTIVITY 2 — A LOCAL LEGEND

Objective:

Students are to invent a local legend.

Procedure:

Most towns have individuals, events, or points of interest that strangers would find fascinating. Ask your students to think of a special person, place, or event in their town or in another town and write about him, her, or it. In their compositions, they should tell who or what the topic is, what his, her or its importance is, and some background about it.

See List 27, Words of Mythology.

List 26. Words of Folklore

Folklore, which includes myths, legends, fairy tales, fables, tall tales, and songs, tells of the lives, traditions, and customs of people. Folklore mixes fantasy with fact and symbolism with reality, and it offers a special glimpse of the people who first told them tales.

admire
backwoods-
man
ballad
belief
boast
brag
brave
calamity
captain
courageous
cowboy
cowgirl
culture
custom
daring
duel
exaggeration
exploits
faithful
fanciful

farmer
fearless
feud
fiddler
fight
fisherman
folly
frontier
frontiersman
fury
hardy
heritage
honor
hunter
independent
Indian
laborer
legend
liar
lonesome
loyal

lumberjack
mighty
miner
miracle
moonshine
mountain
man
myth
outlaw
pioneer
preacher
prospector
railroad man
river pilot
saga
sailor
sayings
sharpshooter
sheepherder
soldier
spirit

squaw
steadfast
steamboat
steelworker
storm
strength
strong
sturdy
superstition
swap
sweetheart
teamster
timber
tough
tradition
trapper
traveler
twister
wild west
Yankee

Sublist — **Who's Who in American Folklore**

Johnny Appleseed — early conservationist

Sam Bass — good outlaw

Judge Roy Bean — frontier judge

Buffalo Bill — frontiersman

Pecos Bill – cowboy

Daniel Boone – frontiersman

Jim Bridger — frontier scout

Strap Buckner — brawler

Paul Bunyan — lumberjack

Kit Carson — frontier scout

Davy Crocket — frontiersman

Wyatt Earp — marshall

Febold Feboldson — pioneer

Mike Fink — frontier scout

John Henry — railroad man

Wild Bill Hickok — frontiersman

Doc Holliday — gunslinging doctor

Mose Humphreys — fireman

Johnny Inkslinger – bookkeeper

Jesse James — outlaw

Calamity Jane — frontier woman

Casey Jones — railroad engineer

Billy the Kid — young outlaw

Joe Magarac — steelman

Annie Oakley — sharpshooter

Old Stormalong — sailor

Pocahontas — Indian woman

Paul Revere — colonial messenger

Sacajawea — Indian guide

John Smith — adventurer

Miles Standish and Priscilla — New World couple

Rip Van Winkle — sleepyhead

NAME _____ DATE _____

INVENTING A FOLK TALE

DIRECTIONS: American folklore often focuses on the occupations and lifestyles of an emerging nation. Think of an occupation of today, invent an imaginary character, and write a modern folk tale about them. Remember that folk tales interweave elements of reality and imagination, and are usually sprinkled with exaggeration. Answering the questions below will help you to organize your thoughts.

1. What occupation did you choose? _____

2. What is your character's name? _____

3. Describe your character: _____

_____

_____

4. How does your character fulfill the duties of this occupation? Describe: _____

_____

_____

5. Is any special training necessary? _____ If yes, what kind? _____

_____

6. In what ways does this occupation benefit people? _____

_____

27

WORDS OF MYTHOLOGY

Teaching Suggestions

Before science, the world was explained through mythology. Most ancient people invented elaborate myths in attempts to explain where they came from and why the world behaved as it did. Although much of our world is now explained by science, myths still make for interesting reading and can provide fine topics for writing.

ACTIVITY 1 — WORKSHEET 27–1, "MODERN MYTHS"

Objective:

Students are to select a topic and write a modern myth.

Procedure:

Distribute List 27 and review it with your students. Briefly discuss the characteristics of myths and emphasize that ancient people invented myths to explain things in nature or behavior that they couldn't explain any other way. Next, hand out Worksheet 27–1. Ask your students to think of a modern problem associated with young people. You might suggest some of the following:

- Why students don't like homework.
- Why younger brothers or sisters like to annoy their older siblings.
- Why teenagers are misunderstood by their parents.

Ask your students to suggest more potential topics. Instruct them to select one of these topics, complete the worksheet to organize their thoughts, and write a modern myth about it. At the end of the activity, you might want to compile a class book of modern mythology.

ACTIVITY 2 — NATURE MYTHS

Objective:

Students are to select a phenomenon in nature and write a myth.

Procedure:

Ask your students to name some phenomena of nature. Some possibilities include rain, violent storms, day and night, snow, and why stars twinkle. Instruct them to select a topic from nature and write a myth explaining why nature behaves in this way.

See List 26, Words of Folklore.

List 27. Words of Mythology

To explain the origin of their world, ancient people invented myths. They told stories of how the world was created, how humans and animals came into being, and how human customs and practices developed. Many myths refer to gods, goddesses, supernatural creatures, and cataclysmic events. Following are some words associated with myths.

afterworld	fairy	leprechauns	sea monsters
Amazons	fate	lightning	shaman
amulet	feat	magic	siren
brownies	fertility	Medusa	sorcerer
centaurs	genie	mermaids	sorceress
chaos	ghost	Minotaur	spell
charm	giant	mysticism	sprites
contest	goblins	Narcissus	supernatural
creation	goddesses	nemesis	taboo
cult	gods	night	test
Cyclops	gremlins	nymphs	thunderbolt
demigod	griffin	odyssey	titan
demon	Hades	oracle	trick
destiny	heaven	Phoenix	trolls
divine	hero	prince	underworld
dragon	heroine	princess	unicorns
dwarf	idol	queen	Valhalla
elves	immortal	quest	witch
epic	incantation	riddle	wizards
evil spirit	king	sacrifice	

120

NAME _____   DATE _____

MODERN MYTHS

DIRECTIONS: Myths are stories invented by ancient people as they attempted to explain the unexplainable. Select a topic or problem such as:

- Why students don't like homework.
- Why your younger brother or sister likes to annoy you.
- Why teenagers are misunderstood by their parents.

Complete this worksheet and then write a modern myth.

1. Describe the problem you'd like to explain with your myth: _____

_____

2. What characters will you use in your myth? _____

_____

_____

3. Describe your characters: _____

_____

_____

_____

4. How will the problem be explained by the myth? _____

_____

_____

28

WORDS OF PLAYS

Teaching Suggestions

Plays are a specially structured form of literature. Since a play is performed on stage, the writer must take into account the visual dramatic appeal of his or her work. This usually requires significant planning and prewriting. Before writing a play, a playwright must carefully consider what he or she wants to say and how to say it. While plays may evolve during the writing process, effective prewriting can make the overall task of writing the play easier.

ACTIVITY — PLAY WRITING

Objective:

Students are to select a topic and write a play of at least one act.

Procedure:

Distribute copies of List 28 and review the words with your students. Explain that plays are a special type of literature and that they have a unique structure. Like any good story, a play revolves around characters and action. In a play, the main character, or protagonist, is confronted with a problem. As the character tries to solve the problem, he or she encounters one or more obstacles that complicates his or her options and compound the problem. At the end, through the character's resources, he or she usually manages to overcome the problem, with the consequence being a happy ending. In some plays, the character is unable to solve the problem, and because of the resulting unhappy ending, the play is called a tragedy.

Before beginning the assignment, hand out Background Sheet 28, which offers a simple formula for plotting a play. Discuss the formula with your students. Emphasize that while a play is composed of parts, all of the parts must be organized into a whole. Everything must lead to the climax.

For the assignment, instruct your students to select a topic—a first date, a school election, the pressures of being a student, a family problem, or a special event. They are then to write a play of at least one act about that topic. Perhaps you can arrange for them to perform some of their plays.

See List 60, Play Format; and List 65, Screenplay Format.

List 28. Words of Plays

Plays are a powerful medium of communication. They enable the playwright to dramatically show his or her interpretation of life to the audience. Drama has a special vocabulary, some of which you'll find below.

acoustics	dialogue	production
act	director	protagonist
action	drama	rehearsal
actor	event	resolution
actress	irony	romance
audience	lead	scene
characters	melodrama	segment
climax	monologue	set
comedy	musical	soliloquy
complications	narrator	stage
conflict	obstacle	star
costumes	playwright	suspense
crisis	plot	theatre
designs	producer	tragedy
		villain

Background Sheet 28. A Simple Structure for a Play

The following outline provides a basic structure for writing a play.

Opening: Background is offered and a description of the situation is given indicating a potential problem.

The problem is revealed.

Plan: The main character devises a plan to solve the problem and achieve a goal.

Obstacle: Obstacles arise that add to the problem; this causes conflict.

Complication: The problem grows and the characters continue trying to solve it. They devise more plans.

Climax: The characters finally solve the problem or realize that they cannot solve it.

Resolution: As a result of solving their problem, the characters achieve their goals; or because they could not solve it, realize that their goals are unattainable.

A play can be expanded to several acts and scenes, but the basic structure remains the same.

29

WORDS OF SCIENCE FICTION AND FANTASY

Teaching Suggestions

Science fiction and fantasy constitute major genres of literature. They are broad categories in which the lines of distinction are often blurred. Indeed, some authors prefer to call the entire realm speculative fiction. For the purposes of this book, two sublists are provided, one for science fiction and the other for fantasy. While the differences between the two can often blend together, science fiction focuses on stories that take place in the future and have a distinct technological setting or theme. Fantasy is more apt to center on wizards, spells, magic, and swordplay.

ACTIVITY 1 — WORKSHEET 29–1, "A STORY ABOUT THE FANTASTIC"

Objective:

Students are to write a science-fiction or fantasy story.

Procedure:

Distribute copies of List 29 and review the words with your students. Discuss the differences between science fiction and fantasy, but point out that some stories do not fit neatly into either category. Also point out that while these stories are about future or magical events and strange places, plotting and characterization must be consistent and believable. Before beginning the activity, hand out Worksheet 29–1. Completion of the worksheet will help students plot their stories.

ACTIVITY 2 — A REVIEW OF SCIENCE FICTION OR FANTASY

Objective:

Students are to write a review of a favorite science-fiction or fantasy story or movie.

Procedure:

Distribute List 29 and briefly review it with your students. The list will provide the vocabulary that they can use in this assignment.

Ask for volunteers to name some memorable science-fiction or fantasy stories or movies. Ask them what they liked about these stories. For the assignment, the students are to select a favorite science-fiction or fantasy story or movie and write a review. Encourage them to include a brief summary of the plot, a description of the characters, and what they felt were the best parts as well as any weaknesses. They should support their ideas with details.

See List 25, Words of Adventure and Romance; List 30, Spy, Detective, and Mystery Words; and List 31, Western Words.

List 29. Words of Science Fiction and Fantasy

Distant worlds and times, magic, and the supernatural compose the realm of speculative fiction. While science fiction and fantasy are often grouped together under this broad term, for clarity and convenience they are presented as separate lists here.

The stories that fall into these categories can fire our imaginations with scenes and visions of the strange, beautiful, and the wonderful. They can expand our horizons by showing us glimpses of what might have been, what might be, or what actually is, although we don't recognize it.

Words of Science Fiction

alien	death ray	interplanetary	mission
android	device	interstellar	moon
Armageddon	dimension	invention	moon base
artificial environment	earth	invisibility	mutant
	enclosed cities	journey	orbit
artificial intelligence	eternity	landing	organism
astronauts	exploration	laser	parallel world
automation	extraterrestrial	life forms	planet
beam	flying saucer	life-support system	planetfall
bionic	force field	light-speed	probe
black hole	future	lost race	raygun
blast off	galactic empires	lost world	reentry
clone	galaxy	lunar colony	robot
computer	gravity	machine	rocket
cosmos	humanoid	malfunction	satellite
creature	intergalactic	mindswap	scientist
cyborg			

space colony	starship	technology	UFO (unidentified flying object)
space drive	submarine world	telepathy	
space station	sun	teleportation	universe
spacesuit	symbiosis	terrestrial	voyage
space warp	takeoff	time travel	
star		time warp	

Words of Fantasy

amulet	exorcism	magic wand	séance
apparition	fairy	medium	seer
armor	familiar	monster	shape-shifting
barbarian	fate	necromancy	shield
beast	fortune	nymph	sorcerer
bewitch	genie	occult	sorceress
binding	ghost	ogre	sorcery
castle	giant	omen	soul
changeling	gnome	oracle	specter
chant	goblin	pentagram	spell
charm	goddesses	phantom	sprite
conjure	gods	pixie	sword
crone	haunt	possess	talisman
deed	hero	potion	troll
demon	incantation	prince	ward
destiny	king	princess	warlock
divination	lance	queen	warrior
dragon	macabre	rite	witch
dryad	magic	ritual	witchcraft
elf	magic carpet	rune	wizard
enchanter	magic lamp		

NAME _____ DATE _____

A STORY ABOUT THE FANTASTIC

DIRECTIONS: Write a science-fiction or fantasy story. First, list your ideas on the simple outline below. Then use those ideas to write your story.

1. Summarize your story in one sentence. _____

_____

2. Briefly describe your main characters: _____

_____

_____

3. List ideas for the opening: _____

_____

_____

4. List ideas for the body: _____

_____

_____

_____

_____

5. List ideas for the climax and conclusion: _____

_____

_____

30

SPY, DETECTIVE, AND MYSTERY WORDS

Teaching Suggestions

One of the reasons spy, detective, and mystery stories have maintained their popularity over the years is the element of reader involvement. Trying to guess who is responsible for the crime or rooting for the hero to outsmart the enemy agents—along with solid action—keeps the reader interested and makes him or her want to find out what happens next. List 30 provides a full vocabulary for spy, detective, and mystery stories.

ACTIVITY 1 — WORKSHEET 30–1, "MAKING A HERO"

Objective:

Students are to create a fictional spy or detective hero.

Procedure:

Distribute copies of List 30 and review the words with your students. It is likely that they will be familiar with most of the words. Explain any that are unfamiliar. Next, ask your students to name some famous spies or detectives in real life, in literature, or on television. It is probable that James Bond, Sherlock Holmes, Miss Marple, J. B. Fletcher, or Mike Hammer will be suggested. For the assignment, tell your students that they will be creating their own spy or detective characters. Completing Worksheet 30–1 will help them develop their characters.

Extension:

You may suggest that your students write a story in which their newly created character plays a lead role.

ACTIVITY 2 — A MYSTERIOUS OCCURENCE

Objective:

Students are to write an account of a mysterious occurrence.

Procedure:

Distribute copies of List 30 and review the words with your students. To start this activity, ask your students if they have ever been involved in, or heard about, a mysterious event. Most people have experienced inexplicable events at one time or another. Instruct your students to write about this event. They should include what happened, when the event occurred, why it happened (if they know), who was involved, and what happened afterward. Perhaps the event remains a mystery.

See List 25, Words of Adventure and Romance; List 29, Words of Science Fiction and Fantasy; and List 31, Western Words.

List 30. Spy, Detective, and Mystery Words

Few stories involve the reader as much as a good spy tale, detective yarn, or mystery. These stories usually allow the reader to become a partner with the hero as he or she tries to solve the crime or outwit the bad guys.

analyze	convict	henchman	private eye
anguish	corpse	hunch	revolver
attorney	corruption	hustler	risk
assassination	court	illegal	robbery
blackmail	crime	innocent	ruthless
bloodstain	criminal	intuition	secret
blowup	deduction	investigate	sentence
bomb	escape	jail	set free
boss	evidence	judge	smuggle
break-in	execution	jury	society
bribe	explosion	justice	solution
brutality	fact	kill	steal
bug	FBI (Federal	law	suicide
burglar	Bureau of	lawyer	surveillance
bust	Investiga-	legal	suspense
caper	tion)	loan shark	syndicate
CIA (Central	fingerprint	mob	theft
Intelli-	gang	money	thief
gence	gangster	morality	threat
Agency)	getaway	motive	trace
client	G-man	murder	trap
clue	godfather	parole	trial
code	government	payoff	vice
conflict	gun	police	victim
conscience	heist	prison	witness

NAME _____   DATE _____

MAKING A HERO

DIRECTIONS: Think about some famous spies or detectives you have read
about or watched in the movies or on
TV. What were they like? What traits
did they have? Create a spy or detective
of your own. Complete this worksheet
and then write a descriptive paragraph
about your spy or detective.

1. What is the name of your spy or detective? _____

   _____

2. Describe the emotional traits of your character: _____

   _____

   _____

   _____

   _____

3. Describe the physical traits of your character: _____

   _____

   _____

   _____

   _____

31

WESTERN WORDS

Teaching Suggestions

The days of the Old West were unique in history. No other country can claim to have had an era that marks the spirit of the pioneers. Stories about the Old West—of marshals staring down gunslingers on dusty streets, of cavalry charges and Indian raids, of settlers staking claim to the rich earth of the prairie—remain popular even in the modern era of computers and high technology.

ACTIVITY 1 — WORKSHEET 31–1, "WRITING A WESTERN"

Objective:

Students are to write a story set in the Old West.

Procedure:

Distribute List 31 and review it with your students. Ask them to think about stories they have read or watched about the Old West. Discuss some of the unique qualities of this era in American history. Next, hand out Worksheet 31–1. Explain to your students that they are to complete the worksheet and then write a story that takes place in the Old West.

ACTIVITY 2 — GOING BACKWARD IN TIME

Objective:

Students are to imagine being a character in the Old West and write an account of what their life would be like.

Procedure:

Hand out List 31 and review it with your students. Ask your students to imagine living in the Old West. What kind of person would they be? Some suggestions include: a marshal, an outlaw, a settler, a trapper, a cowpuncher, an Indian, a dance hall girl, a prospector, or a trail boss on a cattle drive. For this assignment, students are to write a composition describing this person's life.

See List 25, Words of Adventure and Romance; List 29, Words of Science Fiction and Fantasy; and List 30, Spy, Detective, and Mystery Words.

List 31. Western Words

Stories of the Old West are uniquely American. They are a part of our heritage. Proof of their popularity is the great many books and movies that tell of this brief but exciting period in history. Following are words right out of the Old West.

ambush	desperado	marshal	scalp
arrow	draw	maverick	settlement
badge	dude	mountains	settlers
badlands	fistfight	mule	sheriff
bandit	fists	mustang	shootout
blacksmith	fort	noose	six-gun
bluff	frontier	outlaw	six-shooter
boots	gamble	paleface	smoke signals
border	ghost town	palomino	sodbuster
bounty hunter	gold	pioneer	sombrero
brand	gold mine	plains	spurs
bronco	gold rush	pony	squaw
buckboard	gringo	pony express	stagecoach
buffalo	gun	posse	stirrup
buggy	gunfight	prairie	strong box
bullets	gunslinger	prospector	tepee
bushwhack	hang	ranch	tin star
cactus	hayshaker	range	tomahawk
canyon	herd	ranger	town
carriage	hitching post	rawhide	trail
cattle	holdup	reservation	trail boss
cattle drive	holster	reward	trooper
cavalry	hombre	rifle	tumbleweed
corral	homesteader	rodeo	valley
courage	horse	rowdy	wagon
cowboy	Indians	saddle	wagon train
cowgirl	iron horse	saddlehorn	wanted poster
cowpoke	jail	saddle tramp	war chief
cowpuncher	lance	sagebrush	war party
dead	lariat	saloon	water trough
deputy	lasso	savage	wound
desert	lynch		

NAME _____   DATE _____

WRITING A WESTERN

DIRECTIONS: Think of the Old West.
What was it like? You might think of
settlers, cowboys, Indians, gunfights,
cattle drives, and pioneers. Complete
the brief outline below and write a story
that takes place in the Old West.

1. Summarize your story in one sentence: _____

_____

2. Briefly describe your main characters: _____

_____

_____

3. List ideas for the opening: _____

_____

_____

4. List ideas for the body: _____

_____

_____

5. List ideas for the climax and conclusion: _____

_____

_____

section IV

Lists and Activities for Writing Style

32

PHRASES OF ALLITERATION

Teaching Suggestions

Many elements blend together to create an effective writing style. One of these elements is alliteration, the use of two or more words in a phrase or sentence that contain the same beginning sounds. Alliteration can add freshness as well as emphasis to writing. Encourage your students to use alliteration to make their writing distinctive.

ACTIVITY 1 — WORKSHEET 32–1, "MY KIND OF MUSIC"

Objective:

Students are to write a composition describing the type of music they prefer; they are to use at least three examples of alliteration in their compositions.

Procedure:

Distribute copies of List 32 and review the examples of alliteration with your students. Next, ask them to name various types of music and tell which types they like best. Distribute Worksheet 32–1. On the worksheet, students are to list ideas describing the music they enjoy and write at least three alliterative phrases. They are then to write a composition about their favorite type of music.

ACTIVITY 2 — A BIG STORM

Objective:

Students are to write a descriptive account of a storm they encountered; they are to use at least three alliterative phrases in their accounts.

Procedure:

Distribute copies of List 32 and review the examples of alliteration with your students. Ask them to think of a time they experienced a major storm. They might have been caught outside in it, traveled through it, or simply waited for it to pass while they were safe in their homes. Students are to write a descriptive account about this event, including at least three examples of alliteration in their description.

List 32. Phrases of Alliteration

When a writer puts together two or more words that have the same beginning sounds, he or she is using alliteration. While the effective use of alliteration can add freshness and style to your writing, too much of it can be distracting to the reader and thus undermine your ideas. Following are several examples of alliteration.

The little girl received a *big, blue ball* for her birthday.

He *mixed* and *matched* his clothing.

Entering the *burning building,* the firemen rushed to find the trapped occupants.

Brave and *bold,* the warrior approached the king.

She picked the *red, ripe* tomato.

He came up with a *simple solution* to his problem.

The cave was *deep, dark,* and *damp.*

The *crystal clear* sky was *beautiful* to *behold.*

The *salty* breeze of the *sea soothed* him.

The *pug*-nosed *puppy played* all morning.

The *audience applauded after* every song.

Upon blastoff, the *silvery* rocketship *streaked skyward.*

The *deepest* part of the night is a time for the *dark dreams.*

Her *heart* was *hard* and cold.

The *calls* and *cries* of the gulls filled the air.

Prancing playfully, the colt relished his freedom.

The *blaring* of the *buzzer* jolted him from his daydreams.

A *great* orb, the *golden* moon cast its light over the *glen.*

The *cute kitten crept* about the room.

NAME _____   DATE _____

MY KIND OF MUSIC

DIRECTIONS: Alliteration is the use of two or more words containing the same beginning sound in a phrase or sentence. The effective use of alliteration can add freshness and emphasis to your writing.

For this activity, think of some different kinds of music. What kinds do you like best? Rock? Country and Western? Folk? Classical? On the lines below, list some ideas that describe your favorite type of music and include at least three examples of alliteration. Then write a composition describing your type of music.

My kind of music is _____

_____

_____

_____

_____

_____

_____

_____

_____

_____

33

ANALOGIES

Teaching Suggestions

Analogies show relationships. They are valuable to students because they illustrate the connections between things and thus promote logical thinking. They are also important to writing because they can help in the construction of comparisons. Analogies can be used to express various relationships such as cause and effect, parts to wholes, and objects to traits.

ACTIVITY 1 — WORKSHEET 33–1, "CHECK THE RELATIONSHIP"

Objective:

Students will complete a given set of analogies.

Procedure:

Distribute copies of List 33 and review the analogies with your students. Ask volunteers to share some analogies of their own with the class. Discuss some sample analogies, either volunteered by class members or from List 33, and point out what the basis of comparison is for each. For this assignment, students are to complete Worksheet 33–1.

ANSWER KEY: 1. c   2. c   3. a   4. b   5. c   6. c   7. b   8. b

9. c   10. c

ACTIVITY 2 — CREATING ANALOGIES

Objective:

Given a topic, students will generate a list of analogies about it; then students will write a descriptive paragraph about their topic, using at least one of their analogies.

Procedure:

Hand out copies of List 33 and review the analogies with your students. On the board write these topics: home, play, rest, work, and school. Ask your students to volunteer some analogies relating to each topic. Here are some examples:

home — Bread is to toaster as roast is to oven.

play — Bat is to ball as hockey stick is to puck.

rest — Bed is to sleep as couch is to nap.

Using their own experiences for their ideas, students should be able to generate many analogies.

For this assignment, students are to select one of the topics (or a topic of their own) and write at least three analogies. Then they are to write a descriptive paragraph about their topic. They should include their analogies in their paragraphs.

List 33. Analogies

Analogies compare two things and show the relationship between them. They can help you develop your ability to reason. You can figure out an analogy by determining the relationship between the first two words and then find a similar relationship between the next two. Analogies are sometimes written with colons—Uncle : aunt :: actor : _____. This is read: Uncle is to aunt as actor is to _____. The answer is actress.

    Analogies can express many different relationships, including cause and effect, a part to a whole, or a thing and its parts. Following are examples of analogies.

sun : hot :: ice : cold

feather : bird :: hair : human

tigress : cub :: cow : calf

sailor : boat :: driver : truck

sand : beach :: grass : lawn

second : minute :: hour : day

canvas : artist :: paper : writer

tree : root :: house : foundation

bird : wing :: person : arm

ground : sky :: bottom : top

sky : blue :: banana : yellow

hangar : plane :: garage : car

gloomy : dark :: happy : light

town : state :: state : nation

breakfast : morning :: dinner : evening

triangle : three :: square : four

NAME _____   DATE _____

CHECK THE RELATIONSHIP

DIRECTIONS: Analogies compare relationships. Complete the analogies below, then on the back of this sheet write five analogies—each with three possible answers—of your own. See if your friends can complete them correctly.

Remember, analogies are read like this: *Sun* is to *day* as *moon* is to *night*.

1. clock : time :: thermometer : _____
(a) weather   (b) wall   (c) temperature

2. baseball : bat :: tennis ball : _____
(a) field   (b) court   (c) racquet

3. engine : gasoline :: fireplace : _____
(a) wood   (b) brick   (c) chimney

4. singing : songs :: acting : _____
(a) stage   (b) lines   (c) stories

5. pond : lake :: stream : _____
(a) ocean   (b) rain   (c) river

6. sandwich : eat :: milk: _____
(a) cow   (b) white   (c) drink

7. huge : large :: tiny : _____
(a) big   (b) small   (c) enormous

8. poem : stanza :: book : _____
(a) pages   (b) chapter   (c) story

9. fin : fish :: paw : _____
(a) snake   (b) bird   (c) cat

10. boy : father :: girl : _____
(a) lady   (b) woman   (c) mother

34

CLICHÉS

Teaching Suggestions

Clichés are overused phrases or expressions. They have been used countless times in countless stories and have long ago lost their freshness and excitement. They weaken writing by stealing its appeal and originality.

Hyperboles (phrases of exaggeration) and idioms (phrases that function as a single word) are also familiar and may be considered to be clichés. However, hyperboles and idioms, when used skillfully, can enhance writing. They can provide emphasis and make dialogue more realistic. Thus, they are included as sublists.

Students should be aware of clichés and understand that writing riddled with trite, hackneyed, or familiar expressions is at best mediocre. Fortunately, most clichés can be easily corrected. Many can simply be eliminated while others can be rewritten.

ACTIVITY 1 — WORKSHEET 34–1, "THE MAJOR MIX-UP"

Objective:

Students will revise clichés in a given story.

Procedure:

Hand out List 34 and review the examples of clichés with your students. Discuss clichés and point out that many of the ones on the list will be familiar. For this assignment, students are to rewrite the story on the worksheet, revising the clichés.

Answer Key:

Following is a list of clichés that appear in the story. Accept any reasonable revisions of *beyond a shadow of a doubt, to add insult to injury, always there when you really needed her, always willing to help, few and far between, and ripe old age.*

ACTIVITY 2 — MISTAKES PARENTS MAKE

Objective:

Students are to write a composition entitled "Mistakes Parents Make."

Procedure:

Distribute copies of List 34 to your students and review the examples of clichés. Next, ask your students to raise their hands if they feel their parents are perfect. Obviously, no one is perfect; we all make mistakes. Now ask your students to think about mistakes their parents make in their interactions with them. Some mistakes students might think of include: not giving children a chance to explain their actions, feeling that children are too young to make decisions, or not trusting children. For this assignment, students are to write a composition called "Mistakes Parents Make." After completion of their drafts, encourage them to proofread their work carefully and revise any clichés that might have slipped into their writing.

List 34. Clichés

Clichés, sometimes called trite expressions, are waste phrases. They have become familiar and grown stale through too frequent use. They make writing dull and weaken style. Most clichéd phrases can be rewritten in a straightforward manner such as the following:

at death's door—near death
in this day and age—today
hale and hearty—robust

Following is a list of clichés. It is likely that many of them will be familiar, and it is for this reason that you should try to keep them out of your writing.

accidents will happen	eternal triangle
add insult to injury	fair and square
after all is said and done	Father time
a good time was had by all	few and far between
all tuckered out	fond parents
beautiful but dumb	gala occasion
beyond a shadow of a doubt	good greased lightning
bite off more than you can chew	green with envy
blow his stack	grinning from ear to ear
blushing bride	heart in his throat
break the ice	in a jiffy
budding genius	in no uncertain terms
bury the hatchet	in record time
busy as a bee	in this day and age
by the sweat of one's brow	ivory tower
calm before the storm	last but not least
chew the fat	like the back of his hand
clouds of dust	long arm of the law
come on the scene	make a long story short
depths of despair	my lips are sealed
diamond in the rough	needles and pins
discreet silence	nice
doomed to disappointment	none the worse for wear
each and every	no sooner said than done
eagle eye	not a second too soon
easier said than done	on cloud nine

one in a million
only once in a lifetime
on speaking terms
point with pride
quick as a flash
ripe old age
rock bottom prices
sadder but wiser
sealed his fate
sigh of relief
silence reigned
spur of the moment
straight and narrow

supreme sacrifice
sweat bullets
to the bitter end
trials and tribulations
view with alarm
viselike grip
waiting with bated breath
weary bones
white as a sheet
with all his might
word to the wise
wrinkled like a prune
writing on the wall

Sublist — **Hyperboles**

Hyperboles are obvious exaggerations used to emphasize an idea. They can add interest to writing but, unless they are fresh, should be used sparingly. Following are some examples of hyperboles.

I was so scared I nearly *jumped out of my skin*.
His books seemed to *weigh a ton*.
The dish broke into *a million pieces*.
The clown was so funny, *I laughed my head off*.
The wait *took forever*.
After the hike, *I was dying of thirst*.
He was hungry enough *to eat a horse*.
She was so embarrassed that *she died a thousand deaths*.
The dishes were piled *a mile high* in the sink.

The little girl *cried her eyes out.*
He was *frozen to the spot.*
He *sweated bullets* throughout the test.
She was so ashamed that she thought *she'd melt away.*
His heart *skipped a beat* when he heard the scream.
They *waited for what seemed to be a lifetime.*

Sublist — **Idioms**

Idioms are common expressions that arise as language evolves. Usually they cannot be taken literally. To "blow off steam" does not mean that one releases actual steam, but rather lets go of anger or tension. Most idioms need to be understood as meaning a single word. While they are acceptable in informal conversation, under most circumstances you should avoid using them in your writing.

raining cats and dogs	get the show on the road
pulling my leg	over the hill
hold your horses	carrying a torch
put their heads together	out of sight, out of mind
feeling his (or her) oats	start the ball rolling
still up in the air	by the skin of your teeth
throw in the towel	let the cat out of the bag
call it a day	up the creek
stopped dead in his tracks	got a tiger by the tail
hit the spot	rub him (or her) the wrong way
bark up the wrong tree	in the same boat
in a jam	put on the dog
go all out	call onto the carpet
sell like hotcakes	blow off steam
face the music	off his rocker
egging him (or her) on	a ball of fire
it's in the bag	

NAME _____   DATE _____

THE MAJOR MIX-UP

DIRECTIONS: Clichés are phrases that have been used so often in writing that they are familiar to readers. They weaken writing with their staleness. Identify the clichés in the following story and then rewrite the story, revising the clichés.

Jennifer looked impatiently at her watch. Her best friend, Dawn, was late again. Jennifer was sure beyond a shadow of a doubt that Dawn had forgotten that they were supposed to go to the movies. She tried to call Dawn, but the phone was busy. To add insult to injury, Jennifer now had nothing to do.

The more she thought about it, the madder Jennifer became. She decided that she and Dawn were through.

On the other hand, Jennifer thought, Dawn was always there when you really needed her. She was always willing to help whenever someone had a problem. In fact, friends like Dawn were few and far between.

When the phone rang, Jennifer hurried to answer it.

"Dawn, where are you?" she said testily.

When Dawn explained that she had been helping her sister with her homework and that her mother had been on the phone, Jennifer felt ashamed.

"Well, why don't we try to make the second show?" Jennifer asked. She was glad that Dawn agreed.

As she waited for Dawn to come, Jennifer smiled, thinking that they would probably be friends until ripe old age.

35

FIGURES OF SPEECH

Teaching Suggestions

Figures of speech, for example, metaphors, similes, and personification, can add powerful imagery to writing. Metaphors and similes make comparisons. Similes use the words *like, as,* or *than* to signal the comparison, while metaphors do not. Personification is a figure of speech in which nonhuman things are given human qualities.

ACTIVITY 1 — WORKSHEET 35–1, "AN ENJOYABLE DAY"

Objective:

Students are to think of an event they enjoyed and write an account of it; they are to include at least one example of a metaphor, a simile, and personification.

Procedure:

Distribute copies of List 35 and discuss the examples of figures of speech with your students. Ask them to think of an event they thoroughly enjoyed. It might have been a school dance, a football game, a camping trip, a party, or other event. They are to complete the worksheet first and then write a descriptive account of this happy time. Encourage them to use figures of speech in their writing.

ACTIVITY 2 — A NIGHTMARE POEM

Objective:

Students are to write a poem about a nightmare; they are to include at least one example of a metaphor, a simile, and personification in their poems.

Procedure:

Distribute copies of List 35 and review the examples of figures of speech with your students. If you can obtain copies of scary or haunting poems (the work of Edgar Allan Poe is a good example), you might read a few to your students. This will help set the mood. To reduce any apprehension about writing, leave the type of poetry up to your students. Poems can be either rhyming or nonrhyming, and may or may not have a specific meter.

To begin the activity, ask your students to share their scariest nightmares. For the writing, encourage them to include at least one example of each figure of speech. At the end of the activity, you might want to compile a book of *Nightmare Poems*.

List 35. Figures of Speech

Authors can strengthen the power of their imagery through the skillful use of figures of speech.

Metaphors

Metaphors make implied comparisons. They *do not* use the words *like, as,* or *than.*

> He was a lion in war.
> The full moon, sun of the night, shone on his face.
> When he came to the chicken coop, the fox was a thief.
> Winter is a long, dark tunnel connecting summers.
> They were locked in a dark tomb of a cellar.

Similes

Similes make comparisons using the words *like, as* or *than.*

> His eyes flashed like lightning.
> The girl climbed as effortlessly as a monkey.
> She was tired but worked as smoothly as a robot.
> The wind howled like a wounded beast.
> The clouds were as gray as slate.
> He was meaner than a junkyard dog.

Personification

Personification is a figure of speech in which nonhuman things are given human qualities.

> Even the sky cried on the sorrowful day.
> The flower smiled at the sun.
> The mountains guarded the valley.
> The bird sang in happiness at the coming of spring.
> Circling the diver, the shark planned its attack.

NAME _____   DATE _____

AN ENJOYABLE DAY

DIRECTIONS: Think of an event that you found to be enjoyable. Fill out the worksheet, then write an account of "An Enjoyable Day." Include at least one metaphor, one simile, and one personification in your composition.

1. What was your event? _____

_____

2. Where did it take place? _____

_____

3. How did you get there? _____

_____

4. Who was with you? _____

_____

5. What was most memorable about your event? _____

_____

6. Write one of each:

Metaphor: _____

_____

Simile: _____

_____

Personification: _____

_____

36

JARGON

Teaching Suggestions

To be effective, communication must be clear. Perhaps the oldest rule remains the best rule: Keep it simple. As our society has become more complex, however, so has our language. Fifty years ago, phrases like *lunar module, strategic arms,* and *baby boom* were unknown to all except perhaps the most astute visionaries. While this explosion in language has given us the opportunity to communicate as never before, it has also allowed for greater confusion and misrepresentation.

Some people just don't like to communicate. Some try to impress others with their seeming command of language jawbreakers, others deliberately use mile-long words and phrases to obscure ideas, still others believe that their convoluted writing and speaking is good. All of these people, whatever their reason, dabble in jargon.

The phrases of the following list have actually been used in business, government, and education. Clearly they, and similar examples, are not in the best interest of communication and should be avoided by writers and speakers.

ACTIVITY 1 — WORKSHEET 36–1, "PLANNING YOUR FUTURE"

Objective:

Students are to identify the examples of jargon in a given article; they are then to rewrite the article, revising the jargon.

Procedure:

Distribute copies of List 36 to your students and review the examples of jargon. Explain to your students that jargon is confusing because it describes rather than names an idea or object. People may resort to jargon for a variety of reasons—they may want to confuse their listeners or readers, they may think that jargon adds to their stature, or they may simply not know how to communicate their ideas clearly. Whatever the reason, emphasize to your students that jargon should always be avoided.

Distribute Worksheet 36–1. For this assignment, students are to circle the phrases of jargon in the article on the worksheet and then rewrite the article, revising the jargon.

Answer Key:

Following is a list of the phrases of jargon that appear in the story. While you should accept any reasonable revisions, possible revisions include:

> the accumulated skills — the skills
> goal-oriented member of society — a productive person
> a human resource — a worker
> full-schedule human resource — full-time worker
> limited-schedule one — part-time worker
> incomplete success — failure
> philosophically disillusioned — disappointed
> temporary work cessations — layoffs
> personal-directed improvements — self-improvement
> high-order position — good job

ACTIVITY 2 — FUN WITH JARGON

Objective:

Students are to select a topic, generate a list of jargon relating to the topic, and write a paragraph; they are to exchange their paragraphs with a partner and try to guess the meanings of the jargon.

Procedure:

Hand out copies of List 36 and review the examples of jargon with your students. Discuss what jargon is and why it should be avoided. Next, ask them to select a topic—school, sports, dating, and part-time jobs are some ideas—and generate a list of doublespeak phrases that relate to the topic. After they have generated their lists, instruct them to write a paragraph about their topics, including their examples of jargon. When they are finished writing, they are to exchange their paragraphs with a friend and find each other's examples of jargon. Students should then discuss how they could revise their paragraphs to eliminate any jargon.

See List 37, Overblown (Redundant) Phrases.

List 36. Jargon

Language that is not clear is ineffective; it does not communicate ideas. Sometimes, however, speakers and writers forget that simple fact and try instead to express themselves using big words and convoluted sentences. Other writers and speakers deliberately express their ideas in complex and confusing fashion because they may not want people to know what they are talking about. (This is a favorite tactic of some politicians.) Then there are people who believe that others will consider them smart if they use the biggest words they can find. All of these individuals are guilty of using jargon.

The phrases of the following list have actually been used by people in business, government, and education. You should always avoid jargon in your speaking and writing, so beware of using terms like these.

JARGON	INTERPRETATION
administrative aide	secretary
advanced downward adjustment	budget cut
advisory representative	salesperson
aerodynamic personnel decelerator	parachute
career associate scanning professional	store checkout clerk
digital fever computer	thermometer
directive improvement	discipline
downsizing personnel	a layoff
engine redesigner	mechanic
experienced vehicle	used car
fiscally disadvantaged	poor people
food-service operation	restaurant
frame-supported tension structure	a tent
housing units	apartments
human resources	employees
incomplete success	failure

JARGON	INTERPRETATION
limited-schedule human resources	part-time employees
metal cylinder storage container	tin can
misinformation	a lie
misleading information	a lie
nail technician	manicurist
non-goal-oriented member of society	a vagrant
pavement deficiency	pothole
philosophically disillusioned	disappointed
portable hand-held communications inscriber	pencil
pressure garment assembly	spacesuit
safety-related event	accident
security coordinator	a bodyguard
service technician	repairperson
social expression product	a greeting card
temporary work cessation	a layoff
terminal episode	death
therapeutic misadventure	malpractice
time frame	period
unauthorized withdrawal	bank robbery
uncontrolled contact with the ground	crash (of an airplane)
visiting teacher	truant officer
wooden interdental stimulator	toothpick

NAME _____   DATE _____

PLANNING YOUR FUTURE

DIRECTIONS: *Jargon* is a term given to communication that obscures, confounds, and confuses the reader. Jargon is communication at its poorest.

First, circle the examples of jargon in the article below. Then rewrite the article and revise the examples of jargon, making them clear.

It is important to plan your future. Only in that way can you hope to make a proper career

choice in view of the accumulated skills you have attained. By planning effectively, you will

become a goal-oriented member of society.

Of course, you will be a human resource no matter what job you eventually secure. This

will be true whether you are a full-schedule human resource or a limited-schedule one. It is

expected that you will avoid any instances of incomplete success.

In your search for a job, you may at times become philosophically disillusioned. Jobs are

hard to find, especially during times of temporary work cessations.

However, through personal-directed improvements and patience, it is likely that you will

find a high-order position.

37

OVERBLOWN (REDUNDANT) PHRASES

Teaching Suggestions

Overblown phrases are phrases in which several words are used when one or two would suffice. Sometimes the same idea is repeated in an overblown phrase, making it redundant. A good example is *basic fundamentals*. *Basic* and *fundamentals* have similar meanings; the use of one of the words is sufficient. Overblown phrases are instances of overwriting. They clutter writing and obscure ideas, and they should be avoided.

ACTIVITY 1 — WORKSHEET 37–1, "LOST ON MARS"

Objective:

Given a story, students are to identify the overblown phrases; they are then to rewrite the story, revising the overblown phrases.

Procedure:

Hand out copies of List 37, review the examples of overblown phrases, and explain why they should be avoided. Emphasize that, generally, the more concise writing is, the clearer it will be to the reader. Then distribute Worksheet 37–1 and explain the instructions.

Answer Key:

Following is a list of the overblown phrases that appear in the story. While you should accept all reasonable revisions, some possible revisions are:

in an abrupt manner — abruptly
due to the fact — since
in the near future — soon
for the purpose of — to
prior to the date — before
check those facts out — check those facts
all of a sudden — suddenly
in order to — to
lend us assistance — help (or assist) us

ACTIVITY 2 — WORKSHEET 37–2, "THE BIG TEST"

Objective:

Given a story, students are to identify the overblown phrases; they are to rewrite the story, revising the overblown phrases.

Procedure:

Hand out copies of List 37 and review it with your students. Emphasize the importance of concise writing. For the activity, the students are to identify the overblown phrases in the story in Worksheet 37–2, then rewrite the story, revising the overblown phrases. Point out to your students how much tighter and smoother the revised stories will be.

Answer Key:

Following is a list of overblown phrases that appear in the story. While you should accept all possible revisions, some possible revisions are:

biggest in size — biggest
absolutely necessary — necessary
extreme hazard — hazard
killed dead — dead
past experience — experience
serious danger — danger
heartbreaking tragedy — tragedy
think to myself — think

ACTIVITY 3 — IMAGES

Objective:

Students are to imagine a person they would like to be and write a descriptive account of this individual.

Procedure:

Distribute copies of List 37 and review the examples of overblown phrases with your students. For this assignment, ask your students to think of their personalities. What type of people are they? Suggest that they list at least five of their most prominent traits. If they could change any or all of these traits, which ones would they change? Why? Instruct your students to write a composition about their new images. If they say that they would not change anything, ask them to write about why they wouldn't want to change. Encourage them to proofread their work carefully and make sure that they haven't used any overblown phrases.

See List 36, Jargon.

List 37. Overblown (Redundant) Phrases

Some authors muddle their writing with overblown, stuffy phrases in which they add unnecessary words or repeat ideas. Such phrases undermine the writer's purpose, which is to communicate. You should eliminate any excess words or phrases from your writing. The following list offers some overblown phrases that are regularly found in writing and simple ways to correct them.

OVERBLOWN PHRASE	CORRECTION
according to our records	we find
all of a sudden	suddenly
as a matter of fact	fact
as of this writing	yet
at the present time	now, at present
basic fundamentals	fundamentals
be in a position to	can
be kind enough	please
big in size	big
by means of	by, with
climb up	climb
commute back and forth	commute
completely filled	filled
doctor by profession	doctor
due to the fact that	because
during the time that	while
end result	result
exactly the same	the same, identical
exact replica	replica
extreme hazard	hazard
foreign imports	imports
for the purpose	to
in accordance with	by, with
in order to	to
in reference to	about
in relation to	about
in the event that	if
in view of the fact	as
kindly arrange to send	please send
new record	record

OVERBLOWN PHRASE	CORRECTION
none at all	none
on a few occasions	occasionally
on the subject of	about
past history	past
personal friend	friend
postponed until later	postponed
prior to the start of	before
red in color	red
resulting effects	effects
return back	return
serious danger	danger
still persists	persists
successfully completed	completed
ten in number	ten
that there	that
the honest truth	truth
this here	this
thought to himself	thought
totally destroyed	destroyed
totally unanimous	unanimous
under the circumstances	because
until such time	when
whether or not	whether (usually)
with regard to	about

NAME _____ DATE _____

LOST ON MARS

DIRECTIONS: The following story contains several wordy, overblown phrases. First, circle the overblown phrases and then rewrite the story, revising the wordy, overblown phrases.

The trouble came in an abrupt manner, and we had to make an emergency landing on Mars. Due to the fact that our navigational system had malfunctioned as well, we weren't sure where we were. By reviewing maps of Mars, we hoped to locate our position in the near future.

Our mission had been routine: We had explored the moons of Jupiter for the purpose of gathering information. Prior to the date of our exploration, only one ship had scouted the moons. According to their records, nothing was unusual about the moons, but it was our duty to check those facts out.

Now we were stranded. Fortunately, we were able to send a distress signal. All of a sudden we received a transmission from Earth Control. They had received our signal and had already sent a ship in order to lend us assistance. I was relieved about that.

THE BIG TEST

DIRECTIONS: Read the story below and circle the redundant phrases. Remember—redundant phrases contain unnecessary and repetitive ideas. They are examples of weak writing. After identifying the redundant phrases, rewrite the story and revise the redundant phrases.

The history test was the biggest in size that I ever took. And it was the most important of my life. It was absolutely necessary that I pass. Failing would be an extreme hazard to my life. I would be grounded for six months! That would be worse than being killed dead.

As I sat there and watched Mrs. Wilson pass out the test, I wished that I had studied. My past experience in taking history tests was not good. If the past was any guideline for the present, I was in serious danger. I was headed for a heartbreaking tragedy.

I began to think to myself what I would do if I were grounded for six months. The first thought that came to mind wasn't a happy one—I'd have plenty of time to study my history book!

38

SEQUENTIAL WORDS AND PHRASES

Teaching Suggestions

Sequential words and phrases serve several functions. Authors use them to organize information, rank information in order or importance, and indicate chronology. Sequential words and phrases help clarify writing.

ACTIVITY 1 — WORKSHEET 38–1, "A GREAT RESPONSIBILITY"

Objective:

Students are to write a composition describing a responsibility they have.

Procedure:

Hand out copies of List 38 and review the sequential words and phrases with your students. Explain that sequence, or ordering, is vital to writing. In any effective composition, a logical sequence progresses from beginning to end. The proper use of sequential words and phrases will help ensure that the sequence in a composition is correct.

For this assignment, instruct your students to complete the worksheet and then write a composition about an important responsibility they have. Encourage them to use sequential words and phrases in their writing.

ACTIVITY 2 — FOLLOW MY INSTRUCTIONS

Objective:

Students are to select a place they know and write instructions explaining how their friends can get there.

Objective:

Distribute copies of List 38 and review the sequential words and phrases with your students. For this activity, ask your students to select a place they visit—the beach, a park, a restaurant, a library, or similar spot. Starting from their home, they are to write directions explaining to a friend how to get to the selected place.

See List 39, Transitional Words and Phrases.

List 38. Sequential Words and Phrases

Sequential words and phrases are critical to good writing. They help clarify material for the reader by organizing information, indicating that more information is to come, ranking information in a series of importance, or indicating time order. Following are words and phrases of sequence.

additionally	(a) few	next
after	finally	now
afterward	first	on time
always	further	second
another	furthermore	since
as soon as	immediately	subsequently
at once	in addition	then
at the same time	in the first place	thereafter
before	last	third
beforehand	later	until
during	meanwhile	when
earlier	more	while

NAME _____   DATE _____

A GREAT RESPONSIBILITY

DIRECTIONS: Authors can help ensure that their writing is organized by using sequential words and phrases. Think of a responsibility that you have. This responsibility might be household or yard chores, achieving good grades in school, working at a part-time job, watching your younger brother or sister, or a similar activity.

First, answer the questions on this worksheet, then write a composition describing your "Great Responsibility." Be sure to use sequential words and phrases in your writing.

1. What is your great responsibility? _____

_____

2. What are you required to do? _____

_____

_____

3. Do other people depend on you? _____ How? _____

_____

_____

4. How do you feel about your responsibility? _____

_____

_____

5. How do you think others feel about the way you carry out your responsibility? _____

_____

_____

39

TRANSITIONAL WORDS AND PHRASES

Teaching Suggestions

Transitions are words or phrases that link ideas and make writing flow smoothly. They are essential for effective writing. Transitions may connect ideas within paragraphs, link paragraphs, or bridge one scene of a story to the next.

ACTIVITY 1 — WORKSHEET 39–1, "HIGHLIGHTS"

Objective:

Students are to select a time period in their lives and write an account of the important events that occurred.

Procedure:

Distribute copies of List 39 and review the transitional words and phrases with your students. Explain the importance of transitions and emphasize that transitions serve as links between ideas. Without good transitions, a composition would be rough and choppy. Next, instruct your students to select a time period: last week, last month, or even last year. Ask them to think of the highlights of that period. What important events occurred? (If a student claims that he or she had a series of bad things happen, ask him or her to write about these events.) Have them use Worksheet 39–1 to organize their ideas. Encourage them to concentrate on using effective transitions in their compositions.

ACTIVITY 2 — WHY STUDENTS SUCCEED (OR FAIL)

Objective:

Students are to choose either of the topics "Why Students Succeed" or "Why Students Fail" and write a composition.

Procedure:

Distribute copies of List 39 and review the transitional words and phrases with your students. Briefly discuss the importance of transitions. For this assignment, ask your students to select either of the given topics. You might wish to discuss the topics first to stimulate ideas. Next, instruct them to write a composition on their topic, describing their feelings and viewpoints. Encourage them to use good transitions in their compositions.

See List 38, Sequential Words and Phrases.

List 39. Transitional Words and Phrases

Transitions are words, phrases, or sentences that link ideas in a paragraph, or connect one paragraph to another. Sometimes transitions are used to link scenes of a story. They are crucial for smooth writing. Following are common transitional words and phrases.

above	beside	furthermore	on the other hand
accordingly	beyond	however	
additionally	consequently	in addition to	outside
after	contrary to	in fact	rather than
also	different than	inside	similarly
although	due to	instead of	so
another	during	just as	such
as a result	earlier	later	therefore
at last	finally	moreover	through
because	first	much as	thus
before	for example	nevertheless	under
behind	for instance	next	
below	further		

NAME _____   DATE _____

HIGHLIGHTS

DIRECTIONS: Authors use transitions to make their writing smooth. Think of a time period—perhaps last week, last month, or last year—and list the important events that occurred during that time on the lines below. Include some details about each event. Next, write a composition about these events, or highlights, that happened to you during this time period. Be sure to use good transitions in your writing.

Highlight Number One: _____

Details: _____

_____

_____

Highlight Number Two: _____

Details: _____

_____

_____

Highlight Number Three: _____

Details: _____

_____

_____

section V

"Check" Lists and Activities for Writers

40

PREWRITING CHECKLIST

Teaching Suggestions

The writing process consists of several stages. The first stage is prewriting. It consists of various parts, including topic selection, purpose for writing and audience selection, method of delivery, idea generation and combination, focusing of topic, research, and analysis of information and organization. It also includes free writing, which may be the writing of the first draft.

Not all writers adhere to each part of the prewriting process as detailed here; nor do all follow the same prewriting pattern. The value of prewriting is not gained by conforming to a series of steps; but because it helps the writer focus his or her attention on the formulation, development, and organization of ideas for writing a particular piece. Prewriting is the genesis stage during which a variety of ideas are brought together.

Because of its importance to the overall writing process, you may wish to introduce List 40 relatively early in the school year. You may also wish to distribute copies of the Simple Outline Format that accompanies this list to aid your students in organizing and outlining their material. Encourage them to use the prewriting steps and outline on subsequent writing assignments.

When you introduce the Prewriting Checklist, be prepared for moans and groans. Many students loathe prewriting and would rather begin the actual writing immediately, even if they haven't got a single clear idea to write about. Their intention, of course, is to simply get the assignment done. You must emphasize the importance of prewriting to your students and show them how sufficient effort at prewriting will make the overall task of writing easier. Moreover, they will find that their writing improves.

ACTIVITY 1 — WORKSHEET 40–1, "IT'S YOUR PICK"

Objectives:

Students are to select a topic that has personal meaning and write a composition about it.

Procedure:

Distribute copies of List 40, review the steps, and emphasize to your students the importance of prewriting. For this activity, encourage students to select their own topics. For those students who have trouble choosing a topic, offer these suggestions:

How to ask a boy (or girl) for a date
How to keep your birthday party under control
The best advice you can offer your friends
Tips for managing school, work, and fun

Then have them complete worksheet 40–1 and write their composition.

ACTIVITY 2 — CHANGES

Objective:

Students are to write a composition about change and how it affects their lives.

Procedure:

Distribute copies of List 40. Discuss the process of writing in general—there are several stages including prewriting, writing, revision, and publishing—and focus particular attention on prewriting. Discuss the importance of prewriting, then instruct your students to write a composition about how change affects their lives. Encourage your students to develop their own topics; however, you might offer these topics as examples:

How Changing Schools Changed My Life
How Getting Older Is Changing My Life
How My Parents' Divorce Changed Me

Tell your students to develop their topics in accordance with the steps outlined in List 40. You might mention that for some topics they may not need to use all the steps. After they have developed their ideas fully, they should go on to write the draft and then the final copy.

See List 41, Target Audience Checklist; and List 74, The Writing Process.

List 40. Prewriting Checklist

Writing is a process composed of several stages. These stages can be broken down into prewriting, writing, revision, and publishing. Prewriting is the first stage. Just as a builder needs plans and materials to construct a house, an author needs to gather data and organize information before he or she can expect to write clearly and effectively on a topic.

Not all writers use all of the following prewriting activities. For example, some might spend most of their time researching, while others devote more time to combining and listing ideas. However, virtually all authors follow a prewriting plan, although some may do some of the steps in their head. Prewriting is beneficial because it can help generate ideas and clarify thoughts before the actual writing is begun.

Select A Topic

Think about topics you want to write about. Write down possible topics and what you know about them. Do background reading on possible topics. Choose a topic in which you are genuinely interested.

Identify A Purpose And An Audience

Ask yourself what you want to write about on your topic. What is your intention? Do you want to entertain your readers, inform them, or persuade them to accept a particular point of view about an issue? You should also identify your target audience—the specific people for whom you are writing—which will help you focus your ideas.

Choose A Method Of Delivery

Once you have identified your purpose, decide on a method of delivery that will communicate your ideas most effectively. Will you write an informational article, a story, a poem, a play, or an editorial? Knowing what kind of writing you will be doing can help guide you in the research and development of your material.

List Ideas

Working individually, list any words, phrases, or ideas that relate to your topic.

Brainstorm Ideas

Work with a group, if possible. Write down all thoughts or ideas about a topic or issue. Do not judge or attempt to organize the ideas at this point. The objective of brainstorming is to generate as many ideas about a topic as possible.

Connect Ideas

Read through the words, phrases, and details you have listed and brainstormed. Look for connections. How do the ideas and details relate to each other? Are there any particularly interesting groups of information?

Narrow Your Topic

After gaining a broad scope of your topic, narrow it down to one area. What is the most interesting aspect of your topic?

Research

There are several ways you may do research. You may use a library and check books, magazines, newspapers, tapes, or films. You may conduct interviews with people who can provide valuable information on your topic, or you may observe conditions. Whenever you are researching for specific information, take notes and credit material properly to avoid any suggestion of plagiarism.

Analyze Information

As you develop your ideas, analyze your information. Ask yourself the questions *who, what, when, where, why,* and *how.* Think of other questions that might apply. Is any of this information surprising? Has any of it recently changed? The answers may provide important details or aid in the overall development of your material.

Organize Your Information

Depending on the kind of writing you plan, after you have gathered and analyzed your information you may need to organize it so that you can write clearly and logically. Most nonfiction writing should have an opening, a body, and a conclusion. Your method or organization might be a simple list of main ideas and details, or it may be a complex outline.

Free Writing

You can do short free writing early on to generate ideas or long free writing, which may be thought of as the first draft. In either case, write without stopping to reread or correct anything. Keep your hand moving, even if only to write "I can't think of what to write next." Ideas will eventually come and they will often surprise you!

NAME _____   DATE _____

IT'S YOUR PICK

DIRECTIONS: Select a topic that you find meaningful and write a composition about it. Completing this worksheet will help you organize your material.

1. What is your topic? _____

Do you have a title yet? _____ If yes, what is it? _____

_____

2. What is your purpose? _____

3. What will your method of delivery be? _____

4. Would you like to brainstorm ideas with others? _____

If yes, who will make up your group? _____

_____

5. On a separate sheet of paper, list the major ideas about your topic. Look for connections between ideas.

6. Focus your subject into an interesting topic.

7. Will you need to research material? _____ If yes, what sources will you consult?

_____

8. Analyze your information. On a separate sheet of paper, answer the questions *who, what, where, when, why,* and *how* about your topic.

9. Organize your information either in list form or as a simple outline.

10. You are ready to write your first draft!

SIMPLE OUTLINE FORMAT*

Title _____

I. _____

    A. _____

    B. _____

    C. _____

II. _____

    A. _____

    B. _____

    C. _____

III. _____

    A. _____

    B. _____

    C. _____

*Note: Add more main ideas and details as needed.

41

TARGET AUDIENCE CHECKLIST

Teaching Suggestions

An author writes to communicate ideas. The people to whom he or she directs those ideas constitute the audience. When an author knows this audience, he or she can express ideas in a way that is likely to make the most sense to the audience. For instance, you would not explain lightning to a first grader in the same way that you would to a high school senior.

When given a writing assignment, too many students begin working without thinking for whom they are writing. Yet audiences differ. An audience might be other students, parents, or a particular segment of the population. When students identify their target audiences, their writing frequently assumes greater focus because they are directing it to someone specific.

ACTIVITY 1 — WORKSHEET 41–1, "A PERSONAL MESSAGE"

Objective:

Students are to write an editorial on a topic of their choice; they are to identify the target audience for their topic.

Procedure:

Distribute and discuss List 41 with your class. Emphasize the importance of identifying a target audience for their writing. For this assignment, distribute copies of Worksheet 41–1 and instruct your students to select a problem or issue that is meaningful to them. It may be of local, national, or international interest. They are to write an editorial that expresses their views and tries to persuade others to accept their position. While some students may develop topics quickly, others may have trouble. For those students you might suggest the following topics:

> The Use of Animals in Medical Research
> The Food in the School Cafeteria
> School Policy on Student Smoking
> How a Person Can Make a Difference

Completing the worksheet first will help students focus their writing for their target audience.

ACTIVITY 2 — PERSUADING YOUR PEERS

Objective:

Students are to write an article convincing their classmates to support a special event.

Procedure:

Hand out copies of List 41 and review it with your students. For this assignment, ask your students to imagine that they are in charge of a special class event. This event can be a real or imaginary one—a class dance, a fundraiser, a play, or perhaps a class trip to Tahiti. They are to write an article in which they describe the event and persuade their classmates to support it. Encourage the students to follow the guidelines of List 41 as they develop their articles.

See List 40, Prewriting Checklist.

List 41. Target Audience Checklist

Readers are the writer's audience. The writer's ideas come to readers in the form of words on a page and take shape in their minds. Because readers cannot ask questions of an author as they read his or her material, the writing must be as clear as possible. Moreover, because audiences are different, writing must be designed for its intended audience. Following are some questions that will help you focus your writing for specific audiences.

1. Who will my readers be?

2. What is the general age of my readers?

3. What interests do my readers have?

4. What information do I want to share with them?

5. Are they likely to find my material interesting? If yes, why? If no, why not?

6. Do they already know this information? If yes, how can I offer the information in a new, fresh, or insightful way?

7. What would be an interesting opening, one that would immediately grab the attention of my target audience?

8. What details and examples can I use that will make my writing interesting for my target audience?

NAME _____   DATE _____

A PERSONAL MESSAGE

DIRECTIONS: Pick a problem or issue that is meaningful to you. You are to write an editorial that expresses your views and persuades others to accept your position. To help focus your editorial for your intended readers, first complete the questions below.

1. Who will my readers be? _____

2. What is the general age of my readers? _____

3. What interests do my readers have? _____

_____

_____

4. What information do I want to share with them? _____

_____

_____

5. Why is this material important to them? _____

_____

_____

6. What would be an interesting opening to my editorial? _____

_____

_____

7. What details and examples can I use to make my writing interesting to my readers? __

_____

_____

_____

42

CHECKLIST FOR ORGANIZING NONFICTION

Teaching Suggestions

Nonfiction is a major category of writing. It is likely that your students will write far more nonfiction than fiction. List 42 will be helpful to them in the writing of articles, essays, research papers, and book reports, as well as the answering of test questions. Utilizing this list regularly will help students become more proficient in developing their nonfiction writing.

ACTIVITY 1 — WORKSHEET 42–1, "THE PERSON WHO MADE A DIFFERENCE IN MY LIFE"

Objective:

Students are to write a personal account.

Procedure:

Distribute copies of List 42 and discuss the main parts of a nonfiction composition. Explain that virtually all nonfiction—articles, editorials, reports, essays, reviews—follows this basic pattern.

Begin the discussion by noting that as our lives progress we realize that some people have greatly influenced us. Some of these people we know personally—our mother, father, a friend, or relative—while others we know only through what we've read or heard about. These people include authors, historical figures, religious leaders, social leaders, and politicians. Ask your students to think of someone who has influenced them greatly. How have these people influenced them?

Instruct your students to write a personal account of the person who made a difference in their lives. Encourage them to complete worksheet 42–1 to organize their ideas and refer to List 42 as they develop their compositions.

ACTIVITY 2 — GROUP REVIEWING

Objective:

Working in small groups, students are to review magazine articles and identify the major parts of at least three articles.

Procedure:

A few days before doing this activity, you might ask students to bring in magazines from home, or you might ask your school librarian if you can use some of the magazines from the library. You should have several magazines available for each group.

Distribute copies of List 42. Discuss the main parts of articles, then divide your students into groups of three or four. Instruct the students to review the magazines and choose at least three articles. They are to discuss these articles and identify the opening, body, and conclusion. You should circulate during the activity, acting as a resource and encouraging students in their efforts to identify the article parts.

List 42. Checklist For Organizing Nonfiction Writing

The typical work of nonfiction has three parts: the opening, the body, and the conclusion. Keeping these parts in mind as you organize your information can help make the overall writing process easier.

The Opening

- Introduces the subject.
- Captures the reader's interest through the use of a *hook*. A hook may be a startling statement, an interesting fact, a question, a quotation, or an anecdote.
- Leads smoothly into the body.

The Body

- Develops the main ideas with specific details, examples, and facts.
- Answers the questions *who, what, when, where, why,* and *how* for the main ideas (if not already answered in the opening).

The Conclusion

- May contain a final idea, a call for action, or a brief summary of the main idea.

NAME _____   DATE _____

THE PERSON WHO MADE A DIFFERENCE IN MY LIFE

DIRECTIONS: Think of a person who has made a major difference in your life. This individual might be a parent, uncle, aunt, teacher, clergyman, or friend. Use the simple outline form below to help you organize your thoughts, then write an article about this person and how he or she has made a difference in your life. Do *not* use the form to write the draft; use it only to organize information and ideas.

Opening: _____

_____

_____

_____

Body: _____

_____

_____

_____

_____

_____

_____

_____

Conclusion: _____

_____

_____

_____

43

CHECKLIST FOR REVISION

Teaching Suggestions

Revision is a vital part of the writing process. It is the stage of the writing process when ideas take their final shape, style is polished, and mechanics are checked. Revision includes rewriting, editing, and proofreading. A few words or phrases may be changed, or paragraphs or entire pages may be rewritten. Revision might require a new opening, a new closing, substantial cuts or additions, elaboration, a change in viewpoint or structure, a change in sequence, or a new focus. The type and amount of revision varies with each piece. Unfortunately, revision is also one of the more difficult parts of writing to teach. Many students consider their writing done as soon as they place the final period on their papers.

You can reduce much of your students' resistance to revision by treating it as an expected part of every assignment. Revision should come after each draft has been completed. While some revision, of course, will go on as the draft is being written— ideas may change a bit, phrases may be reworked, some experimentation with words may go on—encourage your students to avoid excessive revision during the draft, for this may interfere with creativity. It is during the draft stage that a writer's emotions are often at their keenest level, and excessive revision at this time may disrupt the flow of ideas.

ACTIVITY 1 — WORKSHEET 43–1, "IT'S TOUGH BEING YOUNG"

Objective:

Students are to read a given essay and score it according to a revision rating sheet.

Procedure:

Distribute copies of List 43 to your students, review it, and emphasize the importance of revision. Next, hand out copies of Worksheets 43–1 and 43–2. Explain that students are to read the essay "It's Tough Being Young" and then score it according to the rating sheet. The scoring is simple. Students answer the questions either yes and no. If they answer no, they are to put a reason on the back of the sheet. You might mention that the essay has several weaknesses. After students have rated the essay, they are to tally its score. Point values are explained on the rating sheet.

Now for the fun. Take a poll and ask how many students rated the essay between 1 and 5, 6 and 10, and 11 and 15. (A perfect score is 15.) It's likely you'll get a variety of scores. Discuss the results and ask students to explain their scoring. You might also wish to have students offer some ways to revise the essay. If you use the workshop method in your writing instruction, this provides a way to give the class practice at critiquing an essay before they begin discussing each other's work.

While different people will undoubtedly rate the essay differently, some weaknesses stand out:

- The author doesn't stick to the purpose.
- The opening is weak because no details are offered.
- The author rambles with the development; he or she seems to be writing two different essays.
- There are many short, choppy, incomplete sentences that make the essay rough.
- Ideas are not fully developed.
- There is little logical development.
- The conclusion is weak.

ACTIVITY 2 — REVISE THE ESSAY

Objective:

Students are to rewrite a given essay that has several weaknesses.

Procedure:

You may have the class do this assignment in conjunction with Activity 1, or separately. Review copies of List 43 with your students. Next, hand out copies of the essay "It's Tough Being Young," Worksheet 43–1. Instruct your students to read the essay carefully and revise it. Mention that the essay has several weaknesses and suggest to them that they may find the need to rewrite significantly, adding or deleting material, changing the focus or style. At the end of the assignment, you might display the revised essays so that the students can see how many different ways the same essay can be revised.

(Note: You can use the rating sheet, Worksheet 43–2, with other pieces of writing as well.)

See List 44, Checklist for Revising Fiction; and List 74, The Writing Process.

List 43. Checklist for Revision

Revision is an important part of writing. It consists of rewriting, editing, and proof-reading. Revision will enable you to critically assess your writing and make changes that will improve it. A piece of writing is not done until it has been revised. Use the following questions as a guide for revision.

1. Have I satisfied my purpose for writing? Am I satisfied that I have written what I started out to write?
2. Have I identified my audience and written for it?
3. Does my introduction capture the attention of my readers?
4. Did I develop my ideas logically in the body of my writing?
5. Did I write a conclusion?
6. Did I stick to my topic, or did I stray and include unnecessary information?
7. Have I presented my ideas clearly to my readers?
8. Have I supported my main ideas with specific details and examples?
9. Are my facts accurate?
10. Does each sentence communicate exactly what I want to say?
11. Did I use complete sentences?
12. Did I begin my sentences with capital letters?
13. Did I use correct punctuation?
14. Have I indented my paragraphs?
15. Does each of my paragraphs have only one main idea?
16. Have I used transitions between paragraphs?
17. Have I used correct spelling?
18. Have I used each word correctly?
19. What part of my work can I still improve?
20. What do I like best about this piece?

NAME _____ DATE _____

IT'S TOUGH BEING YOUNG

DIRECTIONS: Read the following essay carefully and rate it according to your revision checklist. Be prepared to support your scoring.

It's tough being young. There are a lot of reasons I feel like that.

I wish I was older. Not old. Older. Say about 25. Then I'd be on my own and I'd be able to do what I want.

I wouldn't have to listen to my parents anymore. I mean I'd be willing to talk to them, but I wouldn't have to do what they told me to. I could make my own decisions.

I wouldn't have to do homework either. I'd be done with school. Forever.

I'd probably have a job—I think I'd like to own my own business. What kind of business? I'm not sure about that. But I'd like to own one. It'd be great being the boss. Giving the orders and things.

I'd have a car, too, if I was older. And I'd be able to go wherever I wanted.

That's why it's tough being young.

NAME _____   DATE _____

REVISION RATING SHEET

Use this sheet to rate nonfiction. Read the piece and answer the following questions yes or no. Give a reason for your no answers on the back of this sheet. When you are done, add up the score. Each yes answer counts for 1 point, and no answers receive 0 points. (For example, if you gave the piece a 3 for question 11, you would add 3 to the total number of yes answers.) A perfect score would be 15.

TITLE: _____

		Yes	No
1.	Has the author written to his or her purpose?	___	___
2.	Has he or she written for a specific audience?	___	___
3.	Does the opening capture attention?	___	___
4.	Are his or her ideas developed logically?	___	___
5.	Did he or she stay on the topic?	___	___
6.	Are the ideas presented clearly?	___	___
7.	Are the main ideas supported with details?	___	___
8.	Were correct mechanics used?	___	___
9.	Was correct spelling used?	___	___
10.	Is the conclusion strong?	___	___

11. On the basis of 1 to 5, with 5 being the highest, I'd rate this piece a _____.

Total Score: _____

44

CHECKLIST FOR REVISING FICTION

Teaching Suggestions

Editors and teachers of writing all too often come across student stories that in a purely mechanical sense are fine, yet lack important elements. For some reason a story may not be fully convincing, the characters may not seem entirely believable, or the story is of the ho-hum, so-what variety—in other words, it lacks conflict and action. The story has no impact.

While a reader, particularly a trained one like an editor or a teacher, can generally spot the weaknesses in a story easily, the task of zeroing in on weaknesses can be difficult for the writer. He or she may be too close to the story and emotionally involved with it to see it objectively. An honest rundown of the questions presented in List 44 can be most useful to these writers as it can help them identify the weaknesses in their stories, which is the first step to effective revision.

ACTIVITY 1 — WORKSHEET 44–1, "THE GUEST"

Objective:

Students are to revise a given story.

Procedure:

Distribute copies of List 44 and discuss it with your students. Emphasize the importance of revision to writing and remind them that revision can include adding and deleting material; writing new openings, better climaxes, and enhancing development; and correcting mechanics.

Next, hand out copies of Worksheet 44–1. Explain the instructions for the worksheet and point out that the story contains various mistakes and weaknesses. Instruct your students to first read the story and identify any parts that need revision. (This can be a small-group or whole-class activity.) Then, on a separate sheet of paper, they are to revise the story.

Answer Key:

Revised stories may vary; following is one possibility:

The Guest

"It's not fair!" Deidre said. "Just when I finally get my own room I have to give it up again."

"I'm sorry, Deidre," her mother said, "but there's no choice. Your grandfather has to live with us until he recovers from his operation."

Although she knew that her mother was right, Deidre was still angry. For years she had waited for her older brother to go to college so that she could have his bedroom. She didn't want to share a bedroom with her younger sister again.

"You don't understand," Deidre said.

"I understand well enough to know that things don't always work out the way we want," her mother said. "This is likely to be harder on Pop than it is on us. He's always been a very independent man."

Deidre was about to say more, but through the living room window she saw the ambulance pull into the driveway. She watched the attendants help her grandfather into the wheelchair. She was surprised at how he had changed. This wasn't the rugged man she had always known.

She felt sorry for him and knew that her mother was right. She hurried to the door.

"Hi, Grandpop," she said. "It's going to be nice having you with us."

ACTIVITY 2 — SELF-EDITING

Objective:

Students are to reread and revise a story they had written previously.

Procedure:

Hand out copies of List 44 and go over with your students the questions on the list. Make sure that they understand what each question refers to. Instruct them to take a story they have already written and review it, answering the questions presented in List 44. Students are to revise any part of their stories that they now feel requires reworking. A new final copy should be produced. At the end of the activity you might ask volunteers to share what they felt was necessary to revise in their papers as well as how they went about revision.

See List 43, Checklist for Revision; and List 74, The Writing Process.

List 44. Checklist for Revising Fiction

The following list can be especially helpful in revising fiction.

1. Is my story believable? Does it make sense?

2. Are my characters realistic? Do they act like real people?

3. Do my characters talk like real people?

4. Do my characters dress like real people during the time my story takes place?

5. Have I used quotation marks to indicate dialogue?

6. Do the actions of my characters arise from their personalities? Do they behave according to their natures?

7. Does my story have conflict, or a problem that must be solved?

8. Are my scenes realistic? Do they paint pictures in the minds of my readers?

9. Does every scene build toward the climax?

10. Is my climax exciting? Is it a natural ending to the development of the story?

11. Does my conclusion tie together all the loose ends of my story?

12. Is my story satisfying?

NAME _____ DATE _____

THE GUEST

DIRECTIONS: Read the following story carefully. It has weaknesses in structure, punctuation, spelling, word usage, capitalization, and sentence construction. Rewrite the story, improving its weaknesses.

"It's not fair!" Deidre said. Just when I finally get my own room I have to give it up again."

"I'm sorry, Deidre," her mother said, "But there's no choice. Your grandfather has to live with us until he recovers from his operation."

She knew that her mother was right, Deidre was still angry. For the past few years she had waited for her older brother to go to college so that she could have his bedroom. She thought of her brother in college now. She imagined that he was having a lot of fun. She didnt want to share a bedroom with her younger sister again.

Deidre said, "you don't understand."

"I understand well enough to know that things don't always work out the way we want," her mother said. "this is likely to be harder on Pop than it is on us. He's always been a very independent man."

Deidre was about to say more, but threw the living room window she saw the ambulance pull into the driveway. She watched the attendants help her grandfather into the wheelchair. She was surprised at he had changed. This was'nt the rugged man she had always known.

She felt sorry for him.

45

PROOFREADING CHECKLIST

Teaching Suggestions

Proofreading requires concentration and an understanding of the mechanics of writing. After a piece has been written and revised, it must be proofread. The purpose of proofreading is to find any remaining errors, usually in mechanics, that might have been overlooked during revisions. Proofreading is difficult for many students, who may not understand the rules of grammar and punctuation.

When teaching proofreading, review with your students the basic rules of mechanics and encourage them to refer to their language texts or stylebooks when they are unsure of a specific rule. Mention that authors often turn to such sources.

While List 45 cannot include all of the rules for mechanics (the list would be far too long), it does include those students will most often need to know when proofreading.

ACTIVITY 1 — WORKSHEET 45–1, "THE NEW KID IN TOWN"

Objective:

Students are to proofread and correct a given story.

Procedure:

Distribute copies of List 45 and review it with your students. Hand out Worksheet 45–1, explain the directions, and emphasize that errors in mechanics will be found in the worksheet. Students are to find these errors, then rewrite the story, correcting the mistakes.

Answer Key:

The New Kid in Town

Jennifer stopped at the corner and looked at her new school. It was enormous. She wanted to turn around and run home.

Jennifer and her parents had moved to Rosemont the day before, and this was to be her first day of school. Jennifer was worried that the kids wouldn't like her and that she wouldn't be able to find her way around.

Gathering her courage—which wasn't easy—she walked the final block and reported to the office. She had registered there yesterday.

"Hello, Jennifer," said the secretary, remembering her. After checking some papers she handed Jennifer a lock for her locker. "Your locker is number ninety-seven. It's down the hall to your left."

Jennifer thanked the woman and left. The halls were crowded, but Jennifer finally found her locker. As she opened it, she heard a friendly voice.

"Hi. My name's Lisa."

Jennifer turned. "Hi," she said, I'm Jennifer Logan."

"Are you new here?" Lisa said with a bright smile.

Jennifer nodded.

"Well, you're going to like it here," Lisa said. "The school's not bad and the kids are super! What's your first class?"

When Jennifer showed Lisa her schedule the other girl said, "We're in the same class. Come on. I'll show you the way."

ACTIVITY 2 — PROOFREADING PRACTICE

Objective:

Students are to proofread a story of their own.

Procedure:

Ask your students to proofread an article or story that they had written previously. Encourage them to look for subtle mistakes in mechanics that might have slipped into work, and which they overlooked during revision.

See List 43, Checklist for Revision; List 44, Checklist for Revising Fiction; and List 74, The Writing Process.

LIST 45. PROOFREADING CHECKLIST

Your writing is *not* finished after revision. You must still proofread your work. The purpose of proofreading is to catch any remaining mistakes in mechanics that you might have overlooked while writing and revising. The following list does *not include* every rule on mechanics, but it provides the basic ones that make a good guide for proofreading. If you are unsure of any rules, consult your language text or a stylebook.

1. Is the ending punctuation correct?

    - periods for declarative sentences
    - question marks for interrogative sentences
    - exclamation marks for sentences that show strong emotion

2. Are periods used for abbreviations?

3. Are commas used correctly?

    - for lists
    - to separate phrases or clauses
    - for dates
    - between city and state
    - after direct address

4. Are semicolons used correctly?

    - to join independent clauses in a sentence

5. Are colons used correctly?

    - to set off a list
    - for time

6. Are quotation marks used correctly?
   Examples:

   - "It is raining," John said.
   - "Is it raining?" John asked.
   - "Since it is raining," John said, "our baseball game will be canceled."
   - "It is raining," John said. "Our baseball game will be canceled."

7. Are verb tenses correct? Are the tenses consistent (no unnecessary shifts between past and present)?

8. Are proper nouns and adjectives, and the beginning of sentences capitalized?

9. Is the spelling correct?

10. Are apostrophes used correctly?

    - for possessive nouns
    - for contractions

NAME _____ DATE _____

THE NEW KID IN TOWN

DIRECTIONS: Read the following story and find the mistakes in mechanics. Rewrite the story correctly on a separate sheet of paper.

Jennifer stopped at the corner and looked at her new school. It was enormous she wanted to turn around and run home.

Jennifer and her parents had moved to Rosemont the day before and this was to be her first day of school Jennifer is worried that the kids wouldn't like her and that she wouldn't be able to find her way around.

Gathering her courage which wasn't easy Jennifer walked the final block and reported to the office. She had registered there yesterday.

"Hello Jennifer," said the secretary, remembering her. After checking some papers she handed Jennifer a lock for her locker. Your locker is number ninety-seven. Its down, the hall to your left."

Jennifer thanked the woman and left. The halls were crowded but Jennifer finally found her locker. As she opened it, she heard a friendly voice.

"Hi. My name's Lisa."

Jennifer turned. "Hi, she said "I'm Jennifer Logan."

"Are you new here?" Lisa said with a bright smile.

Jennifer nodded.

"Well you're going to like it here," Lisa said. "The school's not bad and the kids are super. What's your first class."

When Jennifer showed Lisa her schedule, the other girl said We're in the same class. Come on. I'll show you the way."

section VI

Lists for Reference

46
PROMOTING THE "WRITE" ATMOSPHERE

Establishing a writer's environment in your classroom can be of great help in teaching students to write effectively. Following are some things to consider.

- Promote a positive mental atmosphere in which students are willing to share their ideas.
- Encourage openness, questioning, and analyzing.
- Make your classroom bright and cheerful. Select posters and displays that stimulate the mind.
- Encourage your students to maintain journals and write in them each day.
- Encourage your students to maintain idea folders into which they can log ideas, puzzling questions, newspaper clippings, or just musings that they can refer to later.
- Never accept that students have no ideas for writing.
- Promote an attitude that imagination is an important ability, and like any ability it can be improved through use.
- Encourage experimentation with literary forms.
- Link writing to literature. Let students know that great books are the result of great writing.
- Treat writing as a process composed of several stages: prewriting, drafting, revision, and publishing.
- Provide time for the stages of writing.
- Encourage the acquisition of spelling, grammar, and usage skills within the process of writing.
- If possible, provide a variety of paper, pens, correction fluid, and book-construction materials.
- Provide dictionaries, a thesaurus, a rhyming dictionary, a grammar reference, and a stylebook.
- Encourage your students to write about meaningful topics and subjects.
- Provide a variety of writing experiences.
- Allow students to develop material at their own pace.
- Respond to the individual needs of your students; some will be more advanced than others.

- Be willing to discuss writing with your students.
- Let your students know that you are interested in what they have to say.
- Develop ways to publish and share the writings of your students.
- Make whole-group sharing times an important part of your writing program.
- Always treat writing as an important subject.

47

ANNOTATED LIST OF LIBRARY REFERENCES

In the early grades, most students become familiar with the standard reference works such as dictionaries, thesauruses, encyclopedias, almanacs, and atlases. By sixth grade, most students have completed dozens of worksheets on how to use these sources as well as having used them for reports and projects. Libraries contain a variety of other information sources, however. The following references can be found in most medium-sized and large libraries throughout the country.

Readers' Guide to Periodical Literature

This guide indexes articles published in popular magazines. The user looks up key words to find articles on subjects that he or she is researching. The guide is alphabetically arranged according to subject.

The New York Times Index

This is an index to the articles published in *The New York Times*. You can find information by looking up subjects or key words, such as a person's name. The index provides a brief summary of all the articles published on the topic, giving the date of publication and the page.

Facts on File

This is a weekly summary of important events, trends, and newsworthy items.

The Magazine Index

This is an automated index that includes about 400 general interest magazines. The user is provided with a display of the index on a special microfilm terminal.

Business Periodicals Index

This is an index to articles published in nearly 300 periodicals whose primary focus is business.

The Wall Street Journal Index

This index includes the articles published in *The Wall Street Journal* and *Barron's*. It is divided into a subject index and an index of company names.

Standard and Poor's Register of Corporations, Directors and Executives

This is a leading directory for information on corporations. It consists of three volumes. Volume 1 lists basic information about 45,000 corporations; Volume 2 presents information about directors and executives of those corporations; and Volume 3 is a set of indexes.

Marquis Who's Who Series

There are several volumes to this series. Each offers excellent biographical details of people in a variety of fields. Some of the more popular volumes include: *Who's Who in America, Who's Who in Finance and Industry,* and *Who's Who of American Women.*

Biography Index

This guide identifies sources of information on prominent people in over 2,600 periodicals, books, and other biographical sources, including obituaries.

Current Biography

This is a monthly magazine with articles focusing on people who have recently been highlighted in the news. At the end of the year, the articles are printed in a single volume.

Subject Guide to Books in Print

This guide lists all new and old books currently in print. The information is listed by subject. Virtually all libraries, as well as many bookstores, carry this reference.

Forthcoming Books

This guide lists books that have recently been released or are expected to be released within the next five months. It is helpful when you are looking for current information.

Guinness Book of World Records

This reference is updated each year. It contains old and new world records in hundreds of categories.

Encyclopedia of Associations

Associations can often provide excellent information on specific topics. This guide contains information about associations and how they may be contacted.

In case you still can't find what you need, the two following sources will likely be helpful:

Directory of Directories

This directory offers information about nearly 8,000 different types of special directories.

The New York Times Guide to Reference Materials (revised edition) by Mona McCormick, Times Books, 1985.

If you are having trouble finding the right reference on virtually any topic, this is an excellent guide.

48

BIBLIOGRAPHY FORMAT

Writers use a bibliography to identify the sources they used when writing an article or book. Bibliographic entries are alphabetized according to the authors' last names. The title of the book is next, followed by the place of publication, publisher, and copyright date. If only part of the work were used, page numbers would also be cited. Following are some examples.

Book, one author:
Detz, Joan. *How to Write and Give a Speech*. New York: St. Martin's Press, 1984.

Book, two or three authors:
Ornstein, Robert, and Richard F. Thompson. *The Amazing Brain*. Boston: Houghton Mifflin, 1984, pp. 45–72.

Book, more than three authors:
Dolciani, Mary P., et al. *Algebra: Structure and Method, Book 1*. Boston: Houghton Mifflin, 1980.

Book, a later edition:
Noss, John B. *Man's Religions*. 4th ed. New York: Macmillan, 1970.

Book, edited anthology:
Weintraub, Pamela, ed. *The Omni Interviews*. Boston: Houghton Mifflin, 1984.

Article in a reference book:
"Ecology." *The World Book Encyclopedia*, Vol. E. Chicago: World Book, 1983, pp. 37–38.

Article in a monthly magazine:
Flamsteed, Sam. "When Galaxies Collide." *Discover* (Feb. 1990): 50–57.

Article in a weekly magazine:
Toch, Thomas. "Drafting the Best and Brightest." *U.S. News and World Report* (Jan. 29, 1990): 52.

Article in a daily newspaper:
Chira, Susan. "Electronic Teacher: A Mississippi Experiment." *The New York Times* (Jan. 24, 1990): Al.

Note: Anonymous bibliographical entries begin with the title.

49

FOOTNOTE/ENDNOTE FORMAT

Authors use footnotes or endnotes (notes at the end of a chapter or book instead of at the foot of the page) to identify the sources of quotations, to give credit to the authors of other works, and to provide supplementary information in their work. There are many formats for notes. Sometimes writers will offer complete bibliographical data with their notes. This is especially true when a separate bibliography is not included. When an article, book, or report does contain a bibliography, a practical format to follow includes the author's name, title, and pages.

Book, one author:
Joan Detz, *How to Write and Give a Speech,* p. 56.

Book, two or three authors:
Robert Ornstein and Richard F. Thompson, *The Amazing Brain,* p. 25.

Book, more than three authors:
Mary P. Dolciani et al., *Algebra: Structure and Method, Book 1,* p. 87.

Book, a later edition:
John B. Noss, *Man's Religions,* 4th ed., p.119

Book, edited anthology:
Pamela Weintraub, ed., *The Omni Interviews,* p. 10.

Article in a reference book:
"Ecology," *The World Book Encyclopedia,* Vol. E (1983), p. 37.

Article in a monthly magazine:
Sam Flamsteed, "When Galaxies Collide," *Discover* (Feb. 1990), p. 50.

Article in a weekly magazine:
Thomas Toch, "Drafting the Best and Brightest," *U.S. News and World Report* (Jan. 29, 1990), p. 52.

Article in a daily newspaper:
Susan Chira, "Electronic Teacher: A Mississippi Experiment," *The New York Times* (Jan. 24, 1990), p. Al.

Note: Anonymous footnote/endnote entries begin with the title.

50

BOOKS FOR STUDENTS ABOUT WRITERS AND WRITING

The following books span a variety of age levels. The common feature of them is that they are about authors and writing. Those books followed by a *YA* have been written for young adults, and the reading level on average is appropriate for grades 6 and up. The other titles are more suitable for high school students.

Blotner, Joseph, ed. *Selected Letters of William Faulkner*. New York: Random House, 1978. (YA)

Brizzi, Mary T. *Ann McCaffrey*. Mercer Island, WA: Starmont House, 1986.

Bucknall, Barbara. *Ursula K. LeGuin*. New York: Ungar, 1981.

Clark, Tom. *Jack Kerouac*. San Diego: Harcourt Brace Jovanovich, 1984.

Clark, Tom. *The World of Damon Runyon*. New York: Harper and Row, 1978.

Cleary, Beverly. *A Girl from Yamhill: A Memoir*. New York: William Morrow, 1988. (YA)

Daly, Jay. *Presenting S. E. Hinton*. Boston: Twayne Publishers, 1987.

Donaldson, Scott. *John Cheever*. New York: Random House, 1987.

Dubrovin, Vivian. *Write Your Own Story*. New York: Watts, 1984. (YA)

Elledge, Scott. *E. B. White: A Biography*. New York: Norton, 1984.

Farson Daniel. *The Man Who Wrote Dracula: A Biography of Bram Stoker*. New York: St. Martin's Press, 1975.

Gallo, Donald R., ed. *Speaking for Ourselves: Autobiographical Sketches by Notable Authors of Books by Young Adults*. Urbana, IL: National Council of Teachers of English, 1990.

Gardner, John. *The Art of Fiction: Notes on Craft for Young Writers*. New York: Vintage Books, 1985.

Garson, Helen S. *Truman Capote*. New York: Ungar, 1980.

Greenfeld, Howard. *F. Scott Fitzgerald*. New York: Crown, 1974. (YA)

Haines, Charles. *Edgar Allan Poe: His Writings and Influence*. New York: Watts, 1974. (YA)

Hamilton, Ian. *In Search of J.D. Salinger*. New York: Random House, 1988.

Harmon, Margaret, ed. *Working with Words: Careers for Writers*. Philadelphia: Westminster, 1977. (YA)

Hemingway, Ernest. *The Dangerous Summer*. New York: Scribner, 1985.

Kaplan, Justin. *Mark Twain and His World*. New York: Crescent Books, 1982.

Kingman, Russ. *A Pictorial Life of Jack London*. New York: Crown, 1979.

Lee, Betsy. *Judy Blume's Story*. Minneapolis, MN: Dillon, 1981. (YA)

McKown, Robin. *Mark Twain: Novelist, Humorist, Satirist, Grassroots Historian, and America's Unpaid Goodwill Ambassador at Large*. New York: McGraw-Hill, 1974. (YA)

McNeer, Mary. *America's Mark Twain*. Boston: Houghton, 1962. (YA)

Meigs, Cornelia. *Invincible Louisa*. New York: Scholastic, 1933. (YA)

Morgan, Janet P. *Agatha Christie: A Biography*. New York: Knopf, 1985.

O'Connor, Richard. *Jack London: A Biography*. New York: Little, 1964.

O'Connor, Richard. *John Steinbeck*. New York: McGraw, 1970.

O'Hara, Mary. *Flicka's Friend: The Autobiography of Mary O'Hara*. New York: Putnam, 1982.

O'Reilly, Timothy. *Frank Herbert*. New York: Ungar, 1981. (YA)

Plagemann, Bentz. *How to Write a Story*. New York: Lothrop, Lee and Shephard, 1971. (YA)

Platt, Charles. *Dream Makers: Science Fiction and Fantasy Writers at Work*. New York: Ungar. 1987. (YA)

Powell, David. *What Can I Write About: 7,000 Topics for High School Students*. Urbana, IL: National Council of Teachers of English, 1981.

Reynolds, Michael S. *The Young Hemingway*. New York: Blackwell, 1986.

Sullivan, Wilson. *New England Men of Letters*. New York: Macmillan, 1972. (YA)

Vipont, Elfrida. *Weaver of Dreams: The Girlhood of Charlotte Brontë*. New York: Walck, 1966. (YA)

51

BOOKS AND RESOURCES ABOUT TEACHING WRITING

Writing is one of the most difficult subjects to teach. The following books can help.

Applebee, Arthur. *Writing in the Secondary School.* Urbana, IL: National Council of Teachers of English, 1981.

Atwell, Nancie. *In the Middle: Writing, Reading, and Learning with Adolescents.* Montclair, NJ: Boynton/Cook, 1987.

Calkins, Lucy. *The Art of Teaching Writing.* Portsmouth, NH: Heinemann, 1986.

Carter, Candy. *Idea Seeds.* Whittier, CA: California Association of Teachers of English, 1979.

Elbow, Peter. *Writing with Power: Techniques for Mastering the Writing Process.* New York: Oxford University Press, 1981.

Emig, Janet. *The Web of Meaning.* Montclair, NJ: Boynton/Cook, 1982.

Gordon, Naomi, ed. *Classroom Experiences: The Writing Process in Action.* Portsmouth, NH: Heinemann, 1984.

Graves, Donald H. *Children Want to Write.* Portsmouth, NH: Heinemann, 1982.

Graves, Donald H. *Writing: Teachers and Children at Work.* Portsmouth, NH: Heinemann, 1983.

Graves, Donald H. *A Researcher Learns to Write.* Portsmouth, NH: Heinemann, 1984.

Gunther, Deborah, et al. *Writing: A Sourcebook of Exercises and Assignments.* Reading, MA: Addison-Wesley, 1978.

Hillerich, Robert. *Teaching Children to Write, K–8.* Englewood Cliffs, NJ: Prentice Hall, 1985.

Judy, Stephen N., and Susan Judy. *An Introduction to the Teaching of Writing.* New York: Wiley, 1981.

Koch, Kenneth. *Wishes, Lies, and Dreams: Teaching Children to Write Poetry.* New York: Harper and Row, 1970.

Moffett, James. *Active Voice.* Montclair, NJ: Boynton/Cook, 1981.

Murray, Donald M. *Learning by Teaching: Selected Articles on Writing and Teaching.* Montclair, NJ: Boynton/Cook, 1982.

Muschla, Gary Robert. *Writing Resource Activities Kit: Ready-to-Use Worksheets and Enrichment Lessons for Grades 4–9.* West Nyack: The Center for Applied Research in Education, 1989.

Padgett, Ron, ed. *The Teachers and Writers Handbook of Poetic Forms.* New York: Teachers and Writers Collaborative, 1987.

Perl, Sondra, and Nancy Wilson. *Through Teacher's Eyes: Portraits of Writing Teachers at Work.* Portsmouth, NH: Heinemann, 1986.

Romano, Tom. *Clearing the Way: Working with Teenage Writers.* Portsmouth, NH: Heinemann, 1987.

Temple, Charles A., Ruth G. Nathan and Nancy A. Burris. *The Beginnings of Writing.* Boston: Allyn and Bacon, 1982.

Willis, Meredith Sue. *Personal Fiction Writing: A Guide for Writing from Real Life for Teachers, Students, and Writers.* New York: Teachers and Writers Collaborative, 1984.

Zemelman, Steven, and Harvey Daniels. *A Community of Writers: Teaching Writing in the Junior and Senior High School.* Portsmouth, NH: Heinemann, 1988.

Zinsser, William. *On Writing Well.* New York: Harper and Row, 1985.

52

COMMON FOREIGN WORDS AND PHRASES

The United States has long been known as a melting pot. Immigrants from around the world have come to America with the hope of starting new lives. Although most came with few material possessions, they brought the richest of their traditions, customs, and languages. Over time, many aspects of their former lives were absorbed into the American mainstream. It was like this with language, too. Following is a list of common foreign words and phrases.

adios (Sp.) — goodbye

affair d'amour (Fr.) — a love affair

agent provocateur (Fr.) — an agitator

Agnus Dei (Lat.) — Lamb of God

à la carte (Fr.) — each item on the menu has a separate price

à la mode (Fr.) — served with ice cream; also fashionable

alfresco (It.) — outdoors

alter ego (Lat.) — another side of oneself

antebellum (Lat.) — before the war, especially before the Civil War

au contraire (Fr.) — on the contrary

au revoir (Fr.) — goodbye; until we meet again

beau geste (Fr.) — a good deed

billet-doux (Fr.) — love letters

blitzkrieg (Gr.) — a swift, sudden effort, usually in war

bonjour (Fr.) — good day

bon vivant (Fr.) — a person who has refined tastes

bon voyage (Fr.) — have a nice trip

buenos dias (Sp.) — good morning or good day

buenos noches (Sp.) — good night

caramba (Sp.) — oh my

carte blanche (Fr.) — unlimited authority

caveat emptor (Lat.) — let the buyer beware

circa (Lat.) — about

corpus delicti (Lat.) — the evidence connected with a crime

coup de grâce (Fr.) — a merciful ending blow

coup d état (Fr.) — a political stroke often associated with the overthrow of a government

cul-de-sac (Fr.) — a dead-end

cum laude (Lat.) — with honor or praise

de facto (Lat.) — in fact

de jure (Lat.) — according to the law

de novo (Lat.) — from the beginning

en masse (Fr.) — in a large group

esprit de corps (Fr.) — group spirit

ex post facto (Lat.) — formulated or operating retroactively

fait accompli (Fr.) — an established fact

faux pas (Fr.) — a social blunder

hors d'oeuvre (Fr.) — appetizer

in memoriam (Lat.) — in the memory of

ipso facto (Lat.) — by the fact itself

laissez faire (Fr.) — noninterference, especially regarding trade

magnum opus (Lat.) — a masterpiece

mea culpa (Lat.) — acknowledgment of a personal fault

modus operandi (Lat.) — method of operating

noblesse oblige (Fr.) — honorable behavior which is considered to be the responsibility of people of noble birth or rank

nom de plume (Fr.) — a pen name; pseudonym

non sequitur (Lat.) — something that does not follow

nouveau riche (Fr.) — the newly rich

par excellence (Fr.) — superior; being the highest degree

per annum (Lat.) — annually

per capita (Lat.) — per person

per diem (Lat.) — daily

per se (Lat.) — by itself

persona non grata (Lat.) — an unacceptable person

pièce de résistance (Fr.) — the main dish of a meal; the main thing or event

prima dona (Lat.) — a temperamental and conceited person

prima facie (Lat.) — at first sight

pro tempore (Lat.) — for the time being

quid pro quo (Lat.) — an equal exchange or substitution

résumé (Fr.) — a summary of achievements

rigor mortis (Lat.) — muscular stiffening that follows death

sang-froid (Fr.) — composure

savoir faire (Fr.) — ability to say and do the right thing

sholom aleichim (Heb.) — peace be with you

status quo (Lat.) — the existing condition

terra firma (Lat.) — solid ground

tête-a-tête (Fr.) — together without intrusion by another

tour de force (Fr.) — a feat of great strength

vaya con Dios (Sp.) — farewell

verboten (Gr.) — forbidden

vis-à-vis (Fr.) — one of two things or persons that are opposite or corresponding to each other.

53

MAJOR GENRES OF FICTION

Genre is a broad term that most often refers to either a general classification of writing, such as a novel or poem, or to categories within these classifications. Following are some of the more common genres of fiction.

adventure	historical	romance
comedy	horror	science fiction
drama	inspirational	suspense
ethnic	juvenile	tragedy
experimental	mystery	western
fantasy	occult	young adult

54

GRADING THE WRITING OF YOUR STUDENTS

Grading the writing of students is a difficult task. It is hoped that the following material will make the job easier. General keys to effective grading are discussed first. For those teachers who determine grades on the basis of point totals, the next section contains a breakdown of the major areas of a paper with possible values for each area. A skills chart follows that. Most teachers complete the chart after each assignment and record only major strengths and weaknesses. Skills charts provide an excellent record of progress over the course of a year.

Keys to Effective Grading

- Grading should help rather than hinder.
- Evaluation should not be merely a form of criticism.
- Grades cannot take the place of written suggestions or conferences.
- Evaluation should reflect what has been taught.
- Grading should be based on the whole piece.
- Grading should be consistent from student to student.
- Students should know ahead of time how grades will be determined.
- Report-card grades should be based on an average of a student's best three or four papers. This takes into account that all writers vary in the quality of their work. (You may allow students to select what they consider to be their three or four best papers of the marking period.)

Grading Writing — Point Totals

Some teachers prefer, or are required, to use percentages for grading. Following is a suggestion for how to assign point totals to different parts of a writing activity.

Focus: The topic is clearly defined. (10 pts.)

Content: The student uses fresh, insightful, or original ideas; the ideas are developed and relate to the topic. (25 pts.)

Organization: The piece progresses logically from beginning to end. It possesses an identifiable introduction, body, and conclusion. Main ideas are supported with details. (25 pts.)

Mechanics: Correct punctuation, grammar, usage, spelling, and paragraphing are used. (20 pts.)

Imagery: Precise, colorful words that paint vivid pictures in the mind of the reader are used. (10 pts.)

Style: The overall writing is clear and has a distinct sense of individuality. (10 pts.)

NAME _____ DATE _____

ASSIGNMENT _____ CLASS _____

SKILLS CHART

SKILL	COMMENTS	POINTS
FOCUS		
CONTENT		
ORGANIZATION		
MECHANICS		
IMAGERY		
STYLE		
OTHER		

55

QUESTIONS TO HELP FOCUS WRITING TOPICS

One of the biggest problems young writers have is discovering the full scope of the subjects they choose for writing. Consequently, they don't come to fully know their material, and their writing is limited. The following questions are designed to help authors examine their subjects so that they can understand their material as well as possible, which will enable them to write more effectively on their topics.

1. Examine your subject.

* What is your *angle* or *focus* on the subject? This will guide you in development.
* Define your subject. What exactly is it? What does it include?
* Describe your subject. What is it like? Does it have parts? How is it similar to other things? How it is different from other things?
* Why does your subject exist? What is its purpose? What does it do?
* Why is your subject important? Is it necessary? Why is it worthy for you to write about it?

2. Examine your subject in relation to other things.

* How did your subject develop? Where did it come from? Why does it do what it does?
* What things is your subject connected to? What things does it affect? What things affect it? What changes does it bring about in other things? How does it affect you?
* Is your subject a part of something bigger? How? Do smaller things make it up? How?
* Does your subject follow something? What is it? What comes after your subject?
* Does your subject have an opposite? How does this opposite affect your subject?

3. Examine the value of your subject.

- Does your subject have social value? How?
- Does your subject have economic value? How?
- Does your subject embody any great truths or principles? What are they?
- Why might others want to know about your subject? What meaning might it have for others?

56

COMMON INITIALIZATIONS

As people use language, it is common for some phrases to be utilized much more often than others. When this happens, the initials of the phrase may become used as a short form of speaking or writing the phrase. Not only does this save time, but it allows the phrase to take on added emphasis. Initializations are usually written without periods after the letters.

AKA — also known as

ASAP — as soon as possible

FYI — for your information

GIGO — garbage in, garbage out

HQ — headquarters

IOU — I owe you

LIFO — last in, first out

MIA — missing in action

MYOB — mind your own business

PDQ — pretty darn quick

POW — prisoner of war

RIP — rest in peace

RSVP — répondez s'il vous plaît (please reply)

SASE — self-addressed, stamped envelope

SNAFU — situation normal, all fouled up

SOS — save our ship

SRO — standing room only

SWAK — sealed with a kiss

TGIF — thank God it's Friday

TLC — tender, loving care

VIP — very important person

57

JOBS IN WHICH WRITING IS AN IMPORTANT SKILL

Mention the word *writer*, and most people will think of a person who writes books, stories, or articles. A few might think of someone who writes poetry. Actually, there are many jobs, or in some cases entire fields, in which writing is a vital skill. Following are some of the more common ones, along with the types of writing often needed.

accounting (reports)
advertising (straight ads, brochures, catalogs, radio and TV commercials)
audiovisual writing (filmstrips)
book writing (all subjects)
claims adjustment (research, reviews, reports)
consulting (reports)
copyediting (for books, articles, stories, poems, advertising)
copywriting (advertising, catalogs, book covers, annual reports)
corporate writing (reports, news releases, summaries, manuals)
editing (for books, articles, stories, poems, advertising)
engineering (reports, studies, instructions)
executive in business (reports, summaries, letters)
fund raising (brochures, special programs)
ghostwriting (writing anonymously for someone else)
government (reports, booklets, regulations, statistics, books)

grant writing (letters, proposals, summaries)
guidebook writing (for states, cities, and towns)
law/judicial (decisions, casework)
law enforcement (reports)
lecturing (notes)
literary agency (letters, reviews)
lobbying (reports, editorials, letters)
magazine writing (features, editorials, fillers, stories)
management (reports, summaries, letters, memoranda)
marketing (reports, memoranda, marketing plans)
newscasting (news reports, editorials)
newsletter writing (articles on all subjects)
news reporting (straight news, features, editorials, fillers, obituaries, etc.)
photography (letters, captions, descriptions)
poetry writing (poems on all subjects)

political assistants (news releases, speeches, letters)
professor (articles, books)
public relations (news releases, profiles, letters)
public speaking (notes)
publishing (rewriting, blurbs, proposals, letters, reports, summaries)
research (reports, reviews, articles, books)
résumé writing (concise summaries of job qualifications)
radio (scripts, commercials, fillers)

science (reports, articles, books, grants)
secretary (letters, reports, summaries)
social work (case summaries and reports)
speechwriting (various topics of interest)
teacher (letters, reports, summaries, articles)
technical writing (reports, articles, manuals, instructions)
television (scripts, commercials)

58

MARKETS FOR THE WRITING OF STUDENTS

There are several markets that publish the writing of students. Encourage your students to submit material, but warn them that the competition is keen and that they should send only their best work. Since markets change frequently and some have special guidelines regarding submissions, you should write for guidelines, and, if possible, obtain copies of the publications to study the types of material they accept before sending anything along. Perhaps some of the following are available through your school library. If not, perhaps you can convince the librarian to order them. Seeing the work of other young people can motivate your students to write their best.

Alive for Young Teens, Christian Board of Publication, Box 179, St. Louis, MO 63166. Ages 12–15. Fiction, nonfiction, poetry, puzzles, riddles.

Animal Lovers Magazine, Box 918, New Providence, NJ 07974. Animal-related stories and articles, personal experience, humor.

Boy's Life Magazine, 1325 Walnut Hill Lane, Irving, TX 75062. Articles about interesting ideas, hobbies.

Clubhouse, Box 15, Berrien Springs, MS 49103. Poetry.

Co-Ed Magazine, 50 West 44th St., New York, NY 10036. Poetry.

Creative Kids, Box 6448, Mobile, AL 36660. Grades K–12. Stories, poetry, articles, games, puzzles, reviews, artwork, photography, music.

Cricket, Box 100, LaSalle, IL 61301. Grades 1–8. Poetry, stories, drawings.

The Cricket Magazine for Children, Cricket League, Box 100, LaSalle, IL 61301. Up to age 13. Story contests.

Crusader Magazine, Box 7244, Grand Rapids, MI 49510. Boys, ages 9–14. Articles with a Christian perspective.

Current Consumer, Curriculum Innovations, Inc., 501 Lake Forest Ave., Highwood, IL 60040. Junior and senior high school students. Articles for students with a consumer slant, puzzles, short humor.

Ebony Jr., Johnson Publishing Company, 820 S. Michigan Ave., Chicago, IL 60605. Aimed at black children, ages 6–12. Articles, stories, book and movie reviews, poetry, puzzles, humor, games.

Encore, 1121 Major Ave., NW, Albuquerque, NM 87107. Poetry.

English Journal, 1111 Kenyon Rd., Urbana, IL 61801. Spring Poetry Festival.

Fun, Box 40283, Chicago, IL 60605. Ages 6–12. Stories, poetry, riddles, jokes.

Highlights for Children, 803 Church St., Honesdale, PA 18431. Primary to grade 8. Poetry, short essays, artwork for "Our Own Pages."

It's Our World, 800 Allegheny Ave., Pittsburgh, PA 15233. For children in Catholic schools, ages 6–13. Articles, stories, and poetry.

Just about Me, Ensio Industries, 247 Marlee Ave., Suite 206, Toronto, Ontario, Canada M6B 4B8. Girls, 12–19. Stories, poetry.

Kids Magazine, Box 3041, Grand Central Station, New York, NY 10017. Ages 5–15. Stories, poetry, nonfiction, art, puzzles, games.

Merlyn's Pen, Box 1058, East Greenwich, RI 02818. Grades 7–10. Short stories, poems, reviews, essays, scripts, interviews, novels.

National Council of Teachers of English Promising Young Writers Program, NCTE, 1111 Kenyon Rd., Urbana, IL 61801. Grade 8. Students must be nominated by February. Nominees submit sample of best writing and an impromptu theme written under supervision of teacher. Write for applications.

Purple Cow: Atlanta's Magazine for Kids, 110 E. Andrews Drive, NW, Atlanta, GA 30305. Ages 12–18. Stories, fillers.

Read Magazine, Xerox Publications, 245 Long Hill Rd., Middletown, CT 06457. Grades 7–9. Short stories, poetry, plays, feature articles published once a year in special student issue.

Scholastic Scope Magazine, 50 West 44th St., New York, NY 10036. Grades 7–12. Stories and poems. Frequent writing contests.

Scholastic Writing Awards Program, 50 West 44th St., New York, NY 10036. Grades 7–9. Short stories, poetry, essays, dramatic scripts. Write for current rules. Deadline for submission is January.

Seventeen, 850 Third Ave., New York, NY 10003. Teenagers. Poetry.

Sprint Magazine, Scholastic Magazines, 50 W. 44th St., New York, NY 10036. For preteens. Articles, stories, plays, humor.

Stone Soup, P.O. Box 83, Santa Cruz, CA 95063. Elementary to grade 10. Stories, poetry, essays, photographs, artwork.

Wombat, 365 Ashton Drive, Athens, GA 30606. Ages 6–17. Stories, poetry, puzzles, humor.

Workman Publishing Company, 1 West 39th St., New York, NY 10018. This company has published books by student authors. Write for guidelines before submitting and include a self-addressed envelope.

Young Ambassador, Good News Broadcasting Association, Inc., Box 82808, Lincoln, NE 68501. Ages 12–16. Fillers.

Young Miss, 685 Third Ave., New York, NY 10017. Poetry, opinion pieces.

Young World, The Saturday Evening Post Company, Youth Division, Box 567B, Indianapolis, IN 46206. Ages 10–14. Articles, stories, poetry, puzzles, humor.

In addition, be sure to check local newspapers and local and regional magazines. Such publications often print the material of young people on op–ed pages. Some newspapers will use student articles on school events.

59

PLAGIARISM AND HOW TO AVOID IT

Plagiarism is taking the words or expression of ideas of another author and claiming that they are one's own. It is a type of stealing that applies to all forms of writing and is a violation of the copyright laws.

To avoid plagiarism you should use your own words in your writing and present ideas in fresh ways. When it is necessary to borrow material from other writers, be sure to footnote the material or otherwise attribute it (see List 49 for footnote formats). Always footnote the following:

- *Direct quotes.* Set them off with quotation marks. Never alter direct quotes unless you indicate you have done so.

- *Specific ideas taken from another source.* Even if rewritten in your words, specific ideas should be footnoted.

- *The opinions of others*, whether directly quoted or paraphrased.

- *Any specific display of facts*, such as charts, tables, or diagrams.

60

PLAY FORMAT

Plays are a special form of literature, and they have a special format. Here are some general rules for format,* followed by the beginning of a sample play in which a girl is trying to figure out a way to meet a new boy in school. Her friend offers a suggestion. (Feel free to finish the play).

1. A play begins with a title.
2. A list of characters is necessary.
3. Acts and scenes must be labeled.
4. The setting is decribed. Depending on the play, this may be brief or detailed.
5. AT RISE refers to the action that is happening on the stage as the curtain rises.
6. Character names are typed in capital letters and followed by colons. Stage directions are written in parentheses to make them distinct from the character's words. Dialogue is generally typed single-spaced, with double-spacing between speakers.
7. Longer stage directions or descriptions are usually separated from the dialogue and are singled-spaced.
8. Use the word CURTAIN to indicate the ending of a scene.

---

*The format here is commonly used in schools. Professional playwrights use another, which can be found in books on play writing.

Following is the beginning of a sample play entitled *The First Date*.
   Characters
   Meg, a fifteen-year-old girl
   Jill, her friend
   (Note: More characters would be added)

ACT I

Scene 1

SETTING: Girls' locker room.

AT RISE: Meg and Jill have just finished cheerleading practice. Meg sits on a bench; she looks forlorn. Jill is putting a pompon in her locker.

MEG (dreamily): I wish I could get to know him.

JILL: Who?

MEG: Eric . . . Eric Peters. The new junior. I don't think he knows I'm alive.

JILL: Sure he does. He was staring at you in physics today.

(She closes her locker and turns to Meg; looks at her thoughtfully.)

MEG (frowning): He was looking at the blackboard. I was in his way.

JILL: You'll never get to know him if you keep being so negative.

MEG: It's hard not to be negative when you don't have a chance.

JILL (sympathetically): Well, then we just have to make things more positive. Next week's my birthday party . . .

MEG (curiously): Yeah . . .

JILL: You're coming, right?

MEG: You know that.

JILL: Good, so I'll invite Eric and I'll make sure that I get you together.

MEG: But you don't know him any better than I do.

JILL: That's where being positive comes in. He won't come unless I invite him. (She smiles confidently) Let's go . . .

61

POETRY FORMATS (INTERMEDIATE GRADES)

Poetry is a powerful vehicle through which students can express their emotions and feelings. There are many forms of poetry, the following of which are well suited to students of the intermediate grades. When teaching any form of poetry, you should read and discuss several examples with your students.

Cinquain is a type of Japanese poetry. It is composed of five lines having a specific structure:

Line 1 contains a one-word title.
Line 2 contains two words that describe the title.
Line 3 contains three words that express action about the title.
Line 4 contains four words that express feeling about the title.
Line 5 contains one word that is a synonym for the title.

Because it offers structure but requires no rhyme or meter, cinquain is a fine poetry activity for students.

Puppy,
Bouncey, happy,
Is always playful.
I love my puppy.
Playmate.

Haiku is also a form of Japanese poetry, the original purpose of which was to celebrate nature. Haiku has a specific structure: three lines, with five syllables to the first line, seven to the second, and five to the third.

The bright golden moon
Bathes the glen in its soft light.
It is the night sun.

Limericks are funny, nonsense poems, and they are enjoyable to write. They contain five lines. Lines 1, 2, and 5 rhyme and usually have the same number of syllables. Lines 3 and 4 are shorter (often 5 syllables each) and also rhyme. Limericks have a specific cadence that is easy to learn. Most students like to write limericks because the structure is easy to follow and just about anything is acceptable.

There once was man named McMar,
Who purchased a fancy new car.
He climbed in to go,
In rain, sleet or snow,
But he never could drive very far.

Nonrhyming Poems comprise the greatest amount of written poetry today. Often these poems do not have a specific meter either. This makes them ideal for young poets who can then concentrate on their subjects.

I walked the beach today.
The water and sand were clean.
The air was pure salt.
Will it be like this next year?

Rhyming Poems are common in school. Most children, when asked to write poetry, will automatically begin composing poems that rhyme. Encourage your students to create rhyming lists to help them write rhyming poems.

Spring is my favorite season
For a very simple reason.
Everything begins to grow anew,
And the sun is bright the whole day through.

62

POETRY FORMATS (ADVANCED GRADES)

Poetry is a way of expressing strong feelings and emotions. This expression can take many forms.

Ballad — A narrative that gives the effect of a song. Indeed, many ballads are set to music.

Ballade — A French form of poetry (distinct from the ballad). It consists of three stanzas of eight lines and another stanza of four lines, and is often addressed to an imaginary power. All stanzas of a ballade end with a refrain.

Blank Verse — A form of poetry that is not divided into stanzas and has no end rhyme. Shakespeare's plays and Milton's *Paradise Lost* are examples of blank verse. It is very often written in iambic pentameter.

Couplet — A pair of rhymes that match in length or rhyme, or in both.

Dramatic Poem — A drama expressed in verse. A good example is Shelley's *Prometheus Unbound*.

Epic — A long narrative poem, usually about a historical, religious, or mythological subject. Homer's *Iliad* and *Odyssey* are examples.

Free Verse — A poem that has no identifiable meter or rhyme scheme.

Lyric — A poem that is representational of music in its sound patterns.

Ode — A poem that offers a serious treatment of a profound or weighty subject.

Quatrain — A stanza consisting of four lines.

Quintet — A stanza consisting of five lines.

Septet — A stanza consisting of seven lines.

Sestet — A stanza consisting of six lines.

Sonnet — A poem of fourteen lines divided into various configurations. The Shakespearean (or English) sonnet is composed of three quatrains (typically *abab cdcd efef* in rhyme scheme) followed by a final couplet (*gg*). The Petrarchan (Italian) sonnet contains an octave (usually *abba abba* in rhyme scheme) followed by a sestet (usually *cdcdcd* or *cdecde*).

Tercet — A stanza consisting of three lines.

Triplet — A stanza consisting of three lines that rhyme.

63

EDITOR'S PROOFREADING MARKS

Mark	Meaning	Example
¶	new paragraph	. . . came home. ¶ Next . . .
∧	insert	
	- a letter	comittee (m)
	- a word	They walked ∧ school. (to)
	- a comma	sandwiches ∧ pie, and fruit
⊙	a period	They went home ⊙
↩⊙	move	They went (later) to the store↓
℘	delete	
	- a letter	The be(g)ar growled.
	- a word	He did d̶i̶d̶ his work.
∽	switch	
	- letters	The movie w(sa) great.
	- words	They went (the to) movie.
≡	capitalize	United s̲t̲a̲t̲e̲s̲
/	small letter	The /Actor smiled.
NC	not clear	NC Yesterday they are hiking.
		separate	They went|to school.
⌒	combine	Put on your seat⌒belt.
ⱽ ⱽ	quotation marks	ⱽHello,ⱽ he said.

64

QUOTES ABOUT WRITING

Writing can be a lonely endeavor, understood ultimately only by other writers. The following suggestions, comments, and opinions of noted authors can be a source of inspiration and encouragement.

You must want to *enough*. Enough to take all the rejections, enough to pay the price in disappointment and discouragement while you are learning. Like any other artist you must learn your craft—then you can add all the genius you like.

Phyllis Whitney, *Silversword*

If you would be a writer, first be a reader. Only through the assimilation of ideas, thoughts and philosophies can one begin to focus his own ideas, thoughts and philosophies.

Allan W. Eckert, *The Scarlet Mansion*

Read at least one book a day. Study the memoirs of authors who interest you.

Arthur C. Clarke, *The Songs of the Distant Earth*

You must write what you want to write, staying as close as possible to what the truth is for you, as much of the time as possible.

Judith Arcana, *Every Mother's Son*

Tell the readers a *story*! Because without a story, you are merely using words to prove you can string them together in logical sentences.

Anne McCaffrey, *Stitch in Snow*

'I'll never forget this idea,' is the devil's whisper. Catch everything that matters in your notebook.

Richard Bach, *The Bridge Across Forever*

One must develop his or her individual voice—that's what we call *style*, the name of the writing game.

Judith Crist, *Take Twenty-Two*

If the noun is good and the verb is strong, you almost never need an adjective.

J. Anthony Lukas, *Common Ground*

Books aren't written, they're rewritten. Including your own. It is one of the hardest things to accept, especially after the seventh rewrite hasn't quite done it . . .

Michael Crichton, *Electronic Life*

Be persistent. Editors change; editorial tastes change; markets change. Too many beginning writers give up too easily.

John Jakes, *Love and War*

Weave one's most intimate and secret thoughts and feelings into characterization, a process that invests characters with true life.

Stanley Ellin, *Very Old Money*

Write more, write earlier, write often.

Andrew Greeley, *Patience of a Saint*

Writing is difficult, often painful, and always lonely. As you learn to write better, writing becomes more difficult, more painful, and no less lonely.

Betty Rollin, *Last Wish*

These quotes appeared in the feature "187 Tips from Bestselling Writers" in the September 1986, issue of *Writer's Digest*. They are reprinted by permission of *Writer's Digest*.

65

SCREENPLAY FORMAT

A screenplay is a story written for television or the movies. Following is a format and some of the special vocabulary used to write screenplays. Also included is the beginning of a screenplay, which you may complete.

1. Begin with your title.
2. Acts are numbered.
3. Scenes are numbered.
4. Camera directions and names of characters are capitalized.
5. Character names are centered for dialogue.
6. Dialogue is indented and appears below the character's name. Brief character descriptions appear in parentheses centered below the character's name. Dialogue is single-spaced.
7. Scene descriptions begin at the margin and are single-spaced.
8. Double-spacing is used between scenes, between the words of different characters, and between dialogue and scene descriptions.
9. Acts usually begin with FADE IN and end with FADE OUT.
10. At the conclusion of the screenplay, use THE END.

Sublist—The Vocabulary of Writers of the Big Screen

angle on — the viewpoint of the camera; what the camera is focused on
back to — a return to the previous scene
close-up — a close shot
cut to — to make the picture on one camera give way instantly to the picture on another camera, usually in the changing of one scene to another
dissolve — to make the picture on one camera gradually disappear and replace it with another
dolly — to move the camera toward or away from a scene
ext. — abbreviation for *exterior*, a designation of where a scene takes place
fade in — to make a picture appear gradually
fade out — to make a picture disappear gradually
favoring — a shot that focuses more on one character in a group
insert — a shot of something inserted into the scene, a letter for example
int. — abbreviation for *interior*, a designation of where a scene takes place
long shot — a camera shot of an entire scene

pan — a camera shot that follows action by moving from side to side
pov — a character's point of view; what the character sees
vo — voice over; a scene in which a character's voice is heard but he or she is not seen

Following is the beginning of a sample screenplay.

House of Demons

ACT I

FADE IN:
1 EXT., NIGHT, YARD OF OLD, RUN-DOWN VICTORIAN HOUSE

House is deteriorated with broken windows, sagging porch. In dim moonlight it appears to have been abandoned for many years. The scene is spooky, haunting. The yard is overgrown with weeds, twisted trees, and thorn bushes. Three teenagers, JIMMY WILSON, BRIAN MATHEWS, AND LIZ EDWARDS are standing at the edge of the yard, looking at the house.

2 POV SHOT OF TEENS

LIZ

(nervously)

Let's go. This isn't a good idea.

BRIAN

(calmly)

No . . . according to the legend treasure's in there.

JIMMY

(uncertainly)

Yeah . . . and so are demons. What about those treasure hunters last year? They were lucky to get out of there alive.

BRIAN

You don't really believe that stuff. Old man Carter only claimed that to keep people away while he was still alive. He was a hermit . . . crazy as a loon.

LIZ

But what about the treasure?

BRIAN

Carter inherited it from his father. He never spent a dime.

LIZ

(shaking her head)

The place gives me the creeps.

BRIAN

Look, your dad lost his job. And because of that your folks are going to lose their house. This is a way you can help.

JIMMY

How are you so sure about the treasure?

3 FAVORING BRIAN

BRIAN takes a piece of paper out of his jacket pocket. He opens it.

4 INSERT PAPER

The moonlight shows it to be a map.

5 SHOT OF TEENS, FAVORING BRIAN

BRIAN

(smiling)

This tells us right where the treasure is . . .

66
TOPICS FOR LITERATURE RESEARCH PAPERS

Following are possible topics for literature research papers. Some are general, some are specific, but all can spur the imagination to come up with even more ideas.

The Significance of Poetry

Imagery and the Poem

The Philosophy of Emerson

The History of Science Fiction

The Elements of Fantasy

A Comparison of Science Fiction and Fantasy

Symbolism in Crane's *Red Badge of Courage*

The Philosophy of Thoreau

The Philosophy of Whitman

The Imagery of *The Great Gatsby*

Heroes and Heroines of Literature

Blacks in Literature

Black Writers

The Epic

The Elements of Romance

Literature as a Reflection of Society

Women Authors

The Themes of Edgar Allan Poe

The Impact of Emerson on Thoreau's Ideas of Nature

Alienation in Fitzgerald's *Great Gatsby*

Individualism in the Writings of Emerson

The Development of the Protagonist in Hemingway's *The Sun Also Rises*

The Epic Elements of *Moby Dick*

A Comparison of Style and Technique in Crane's *Red Badge of Courage* and Heller's *Catch-22*

The Elements of the Mystery

The Great Mystery Writers

How Agatha Christie Builds Suspense

In addition, authors and their works can be excellent subjects for research papers. This is a short sampling of classic or well-known authors and one of their works that is geared more to the high school student.

Maya Angelou, *I Know Why the Caged Bird Sings*

Isaac Asimov, *Foundation Trilogy*

Jane Austen, *Pride and Prejudice*

James Baldwin, *Notes of a Native Son*

Emily Brontë, *Wuthering Heights*

Pearl Buck, *The Good Earth*

Edgar Rice Burroughs, *Tarzan*

Truman Capote, *In Cold Blood*

Stephen Crane, *Red Badge of Courage*

Ralph Ellison, *The Invisible Man*

William Faulkner, *The Sound and the Fury*

F. Scott Fitzgerald, *The Great Gatsby*

William Golding, *Lord of the Flies*

Joseph Heller, *Catch 22*

Ernest Hemingway, *A Farewell to Arms*

John Hersey, *Hiroshima*

Aldous Huxley, *Brave New World*

Jack Kerouac, *On the Road*

Ken Kesey, *One Flew Over the Cuckoo's Nest*

Rudyard Kipling, *Captains Courageous*

John Knowles, *A Separate Peace*

Ursula K. LeGuin, *The Left Hand of Darkness*

Ira Levin, *Rosemary's Baby*

Bernard Malamud, *The Natural*

Carson McCullers, *The Member of the Wedding*

Margaret Mitchell, *Gone with the Wind*

James Michener, *Texas*

George Orwell, *1984*

Sylvia Plath, *The Bell Jar*

Philip Roth, *Portnoy's Complaint*

J.D. Salinger, *The Catcher in the Rye*

John Steinbeck, *The Grapes of Wrath*

Robert Louis Stevenson, *The Strange Case of Dr. Jekyll and Mr. Hyde*

Harriet Beecher Stowe, *Uncle Tom's Cabin*

Mark Twain, *The Adventures of Huckleberry Finn*

Anne Tyler, *Dinner at the Homesick Restaurant*

John Updike, *Rabbit Run*

Kurt Vonnegut, *Slaughterhouse Five*

Alice Walker, *The Color Purple*

Robert Penn Warren, *All the King's Men*

Richard Wright, *Native Son*

The following titles are especially popular among junior high and upper elementary students.

Louisa May Alcott, *Little Women*

Judy Blume, *Just As Long As We're Together*

Betsy Byars, *The Summer of the Swans*

Beverly Cleary, *Fifteen*

Eleanor Clymer, *My Brother Stevie*

Scott Corbett, *The Lemonade Trick*

Roald Dahl, *Charlie and the Chocolate Factory*

Howard Fast, *April Morning*

Sid Fleischman, *The Whipping Boy*

S. E. Hinton, *Taming the Star Runner*

Virginia Hamilton, *The House of Dies Drear*

Irene Hunt, *No Promises in the Wind*

Norma Klein, *Mom, the Wolf Man and Me*

Elizabeth Levy, *Lizzie Lies a Lot*

Robert Lipsyte, *One Fat Summer*

Joan Lowery Nixon, *And Maggie Makes Three*

Robert C. O'Brien, *Mrs. Frisby and the Rats of NIMH*

Scott O'Dell, *Sing Down the Moon*

Barbara Park, *Beanpole*

Katherine Paterson, *Bridge to Terabithia*

Gary Paulsen, *Hatchet*

J.R.R. Tolkien, *The Hobbit*

Cynthia Voigt, *Dicey's Song*

Paul Zindel, *Confessions of a Teenage Baboon*

Following are some topics for poetry.

The Images of Plath's "Fever 103"

The Folk Traditions of the Poetry of Langston Hughes

A Comparison of the Use of Nature in the Poems of Emily Dickinson and Robert Frost

The Theme of Death in the Poetry of Edgar Allan Poe

The Imagery of the Poems of William Carlos Williams

The Philosophy of Wordsworth Through his Poetry

Imagery in Romantic Poetry

Satire in Poetry

The Influence of Carl Sandburg's Life on His Poetry

The Elements of Epic Poems

The Interpretation of Ginsberg's "Howl"

As an added resource, you might check the National Council of Teachers of English *Books for You: A Booklist for Senior High Students*, edited by Abrahamson and Carter, 1988. For younger students, consult NCTE's *Your Reading: A Booklist for Junior High and Middle School Students*, 7th ed., edited by Davis and Davis, 1988.

67

STEPS FOR DOING A RESEARCH PAPER

Following are nine steps that can act as guideposts in the completion of a research paper.

1. Select and limit your subject. Choose a subject that you find interesting, then do general background reading to gain a feel for the scope of the material. Narrow your subject down to a well-focused topic.

2. Decide what sources you will need. Will you require books, magazines, interviews, or forms of nonprint media such as tapes or photographs? Where will you find these sources?

3. Prepare a preliminary outline. This may be merely a list of the main ideas or topics that will appear in your paper, but it will provide you with direction in your research efforts.

4. Conduct your research. Take accurate notes, and record your sources, including page references. This will save much time later.

5. Review your notes. Analyze, combine, and organize your data. If necessary, conduct further research.

6. Organize your information into an outline. Remember that every research paper consists of three basic parts: an introduction, a body, and a conclusion.

7. Write your first draft. Rely on your outline for this.

8. Review your draft and revise it. Make any additions or deletions as well as polish the writing.

9. Write the final draft, making any final changes. Include footnotes and a bibliography.

When using a word processor or typewriter, use 8½″ × 11″ white paper, print on only one side with black ink, and use double-spacing. Extended quotes should be single-spaced. Be sure to leave ample margins.

68

TYPES OF WRITING

If we are not careful, we can fall into the habit of writing about the same types of topics. Actually, there are many kinds of writing that can easily be done in the classroom.

advertisements

advice columns

allegories

anecdotes

autobiographies

awards

ballads

biographies

book reviews

cartoons

comic strips

diaries

editorials

essays

fables

fairy tales

fiction (adventure, contemporary,
	fantasy, historical, mystery,
	romance, science fiction)

folk tales

greeting cards

how-to articles

informational articles

instructions

interviews

jokes

journals

letters (apology, business,
	complaint, congratulation,
	friendly, job application,
	to the editor)

movie reviews

myths

newspaper articles

plays

poetry (nonrhyme, rhyme, special
	types including cinquain,
	haiku, limericks)

puzzles

quizzes

radio scripts

research papers

résumés

speeches

tall tales

TV scripts

69

WRITING ACTIVITIES FOR OTHER SUBJECTS

Writing should be a significant part of every class, not just language arts. Indeed, the teaching of effective writing should be a school goal. When a school is committed to writing instruction, students gain significant exposure to writing forms and purposes. Every class can incorporate writing into its routines and lessons. Following is a list of activities.

Writing for Art

- Paint self-portraits and write autobiographical sketches.
- Draw and describe in writing imaginary creatures.
- Write an article about moods and colors.
- Write an article about photography as a form of art.
- Create comic strips, either of favorite or new characters.
- Design an imaginary object using clay or another material. Then write a story about it.
- Produce an object and write a set of instructions explaining how others can make it.
- Make puppets, write a script for a puppet show, and perform the show.
- Make a collage depicting an issue that has personal meaning and write an essay on the topic.
- Write and illustrate a tall tale.
- Write a science-fiction story. Illustrate it or create an object that depicts some part of the story.

Writing for Math

- Select famous mathematicians. Pythagoras is an example. Write biographies about the lives of these people, focusing on their mathematical accomplishments. Perhaps the biographies can be compiled into a class book of Famous Mathematicians.
- Create computer programs, then write manuals explaining how to use the program.
- Write an article entitled "Math and Recordkeeping."

- Write word problems that other students solve. (This can be done throughout the year as different topics are covered.)
- Write articles about how mathematics affects our lives.
- Select a geometric figure—a square, triangle, or rectangle, for example—and write a poem or story about it.
- Create a math word find, using at least twelve math words. (Hint: Graph paper makes it easier to create word finds.)
- Pretend to be a math teacher. Convince your students that math is important. What would you say? Write an essay convincing others of the importance of math.

Writing for Music

- Write a biography of a famous composer.
- Write songs and lyrics. (Your class may conduct a school song-writing contest.)
- Choose a favorite pop singer. Imagine being able to go on tour with this star. What would it be like? Write an account of this imaginary experience.
- Write, create, and perform your own rock videos. (Your class may wish to tape the best ones or conduct a contest.)
- Write an editorial on why you should or should not be permitted to listen to the type of music you like.
- Select a type of music and write a report about it including its origin, where it is most often played, and its unique elements.

Writing for Reading

- Select a favorite story and write a summary of it.
- Write book reviews. (Your class may compile the reviews and use them in the selection of new books to read.)
- Read a play, then write a play of your own on a topic of your choice. (Your teacher may allow students to create the props and act out their plays.)
- Choose a favorite character and write a poem describing this character.
- Write biographies of famous authors.
- Select a favorite story and write a new ending for it.
- Write essays comparing reading and television.

Writing for Science

- Write a research report comparing science and superstition.
- Write an article about the importance of a balanced diet.
- Write a story based on a topic you have studied or are currently studying.
- Choose a mystery—some examples are UFOs, Bigfoot, the Loch Ness monster, and ghosts—conduct the necessary research, and write a report.
- Pretend to be a scientist and plan a trip to another planet. Describe your preparations in an essay or story.
- Imagine that aliens have made contact with earth. Write an imaginary interview with the first alien to land on earth.
- Select a famous scientist from the area you are studying and write a biographical sketch.
- Create a model of a topic in science and write a description of it.
- Write a report entitled "Modern Methods in Weather Forecasting."
- Write articles describing possible energy sources of the future.
- Write a proposal for an experiment, detailing each step of the scientific process, particularly hypothesis, procedure, and controls.
- Write a summary of the results of an experiment.

Writing for Social Studies

- Select a historical event, imagine you are a reporter at the scene, and write a news story describing the event.
- Select a favorite product, and write a description of why it is good and worthwhile.
- Write a brochure that describes your town or neighborhood.
- Choose a topic of major importance—poverty, homelessness, drug abuse—and write a report examining potential solutions.
- Imagine that time travel is possible. Write a travel brochure describing a vacation spot from the past.
- Select a problem or issue that is meaningful to you and write an editorial about it.
- Research and write a biography about a major historical figure you admire.
- Select a country that one or more of your ancestors came from. Compare that country with the United States.

70

WAYS TO PUBLISH THE WORK OF YOUR STUDENTS

There are many ways to share, or publish, the writing of your students.

- Reading student work out loud in class

- Bulletin boards in class

- Hallway displays

- Holding "readings" in assemblies or special programs

- Publication in class or school magazines or newsletters

- Publication in PTA newsletters

- Sharing writing with parents and asking for written comments

- Photocopying compositions and sharing with other students

- Presenting writing to students of other classes

- Producing class books of selected writing

- Developing anthologies of student writing and displaying them in the school or local library

- Submitting student writing to local newspapers

- Submitting student writing to magazines that publish the writing of students

71

TIPS FOR ANSWERING ESSAY TESTS

Every student is faced with essay tests. The following suggestions can help students answer those questions effectively.

1. Read the question carefully. Make sure you know exactly what it is asking. Look for key words such as *summarize, describe, explain, compare, contrast, analyze,* and *discuss.*

2. Write your ideas down on scrap paper. As you do, look for connections and relationships between ideas.

3. Organize your ideas in a logical manner. Compose a simple list that can serve as an outline.

4. Write your essay, referring to your idea list. Be sure to use an introduction, body, and conclusion. You should state your argument or viewpoint in the introduction, develop your ideas in the body, and offer a final statement of your position in the conclusion. Keep your writing concise.

5. Review your answer. Although you may not have much time for revision, use the time you do have for making your ideas as clear as possible and polishing your writing.

72

GUIDELINES FOR WRITER'S CONFERENCES

The writer's conference is a time for teaching and learning. Following are some suggestions to help you make your conferences more effective.

1. Set up a schedule and follow it. Some teachers prefer to meet with students after every assignment while others prefer to meet regularly once every week or every two weeks. Adhering to a schedule allows both teacher and student to plan on the meeting.

2. Meet in a corner of the room, at your desk, at the student's desk, or in some other designated area.

3. If possible, begin the conference by asking your students what they wish to focus on. This is especially helpful when discussing a work in progress.

4. Keep your conferences short. Two to three minutes is usually sufficient. Rather than reading the entire piece during the conference, try to read it earlier and make notes. Use the conference time for talking and sharing.

5. Focus on one or two specific strengths and weaknesses of the piece. It is impossible to talk about the entire piece; even if you tried, you would likely overwhelm your students.

6. See every student. If you can't get to everyone one day, make sure you do it the next.

7. Be sincere and specific in your praise. Students can see through false praise. When offering compliments on their writing, point out particular strengths. "Your imagery is strong. I can picture that old house clearly."

8. Be helpful with criticism. Avoid negative or sarcastic comments and instead use criticism as a way to help students improve their writing skills. Rather than, "Your dialogue is poor because it lacks quotation marks," say, "The reader needs to know when characters are speaking. The writer does this by using quotation marks."

9. Base your suggestions for improvement on skills that the student knows. Build on mastered skills.

10. Remember to listen to your students. Don't make the conference a one-way street. Ask students how they feel they might be able to improve the piece. What did they like best? What did they like the least? What do they like about their writing? How do they feel they can improve? Establish a dialogue with your students so that they become partners with you in the development of their writing skills.

73

WRITER'S GLOSSARY

Like other professions, writing has a special vocabulary, words that are unique to its field. Here are some.

advance — money paid to a writer by a publisher before a book is published; the money is charged against the royalties that the book will earn

assignment — situation in which an editor asks an author to write a specific article, story, or book

author's tour — a "tour" in which an author visits various cities to promote a book

B & W — an abbreviation for black-and-white photographs

bimonthly — a publication that comes out every two weeks

bionote — a sentence or short paragraph about an author that appears at the beginning of his or her article or story

blurb — a brief publicity notice on a book jacket designed to arouse interest

caption — a written description of a photograph

clean copy — a manuscript that is free of errors and cross-outs

clips — samples of a writer's published work

column inch — the type contained in one inch of a typeset column

contributor's copies — copies of a magazine sent to an author in which his or her work appears

copy — a manuscript; also may refer to written material

copyediting — the editing of a manuscript for mechanics—grammar, punctuation, and spelling—as well as for printing style

copywriting — the writing of material for advertising

cover letter — a brief letter that accompanies the submission of a manuscript

desktop publishing — publishing done using a personal computer

docudrama — a fictionalized film based on actual, usually recent, events and real people

editor — a person who accepts or rejects manuscripts for publication; editors also ensure that accepted manuscripts are prepared for publication

fair use — a provision of the copyright law that allows brief passages from copyrighted material to be used without violating the owner's rights

feature — a lead article in a magazine

filler — a short item used to "fill" leftover space in a magazine or newspaper

freelance — a situation in which an author sells his or her material to various publishers

genre — a classification of writing; science fiction, for example, is a genre

ghostwriter — a writer who anonymously writes a book, article, or story for another

glossy — a black-and-white photograph with a shiny surface

how-to — a book or article that explains how to do something

illustrations — photographs, artwork, or engravings that accompany a manuscript

interactive fiction — stories in which the reader chooses the way a story develops

kill fee — the fee for an article that was assigned and written but was not used

mainstream fiction — popular fiction such as romance, mystery, or science fiction

manuscript — a typed (prepublication) copy of a book, article, story, or poem

multiple submissions — the act of sending the same manuscript to several publishers at the same time

newsbreak — an important story added to the front page of a newspaper or magazine at press time

novel — a fictional book

novella — a short novel

paperback — a book that has a flexible paper binding

payment on acceptance — a payment method in which a publisher pays a writer on the editor's acceptance of the writer's work

payment on publication — a payment method in which the writer is paid when his or her material is published

pen name — a name other than his or her own that an author uses for publication (also, *nom de plume* or *pseudonym*)

permission — a written consent that grants an author the right to use material originally published by another writer

photo feature — an article in which the emphasis is on photographs rather than written material

plagiarism — the taking of the work of another writer and calling it one's own (or implying that it is one's own by not attributing it to another source)

print run — the number of books produced at a given printing

proofreading — reading a manuscript carefully to correct errors in mechanics

proposal — a portion of a book used to interest a publisher, typically including an outline and sample chapter(s)

public domain — material on which the copyright term has expired or material that was never copyrighted

publisher — an individual or company that prints articles, stories, books, or poems

query — a letter sent to an editor by a writer in which the writer tries to interest the editor in an article idea

rejection — the unhappy situation that occurs when an editor decides not to accept or purchase a manuscript

royalties — payment to an author based on the amount of sales his or her book has achieved

screenplay — a story written in a movie or TV format

semimonthly — a magazine that comes out twice a month

serial — a newspaper or magazine (also stories in them) that appear at periodic intervals

sidebar — an additional, usually short, article that accompanies and highlights a feature

slant — the design or development of an article or story that makes it particularly suited to a target audience

slush pile — the pile of unsolicited manuscripts received by an editor or publisher

speculation — a situation in which an editor agrees to look at a manuscript with no commitment that he or she will buy it; often referred to as "on spec"

submission — the act of sending a manuscript to an editor

subsidiary rights (subrights) — rights distinct from book publishing rights included in a book contract; subrights may include paperback, book club, and movie rights

synopsis — a brief summary of a novel, story, or play

tagline — a comment added to a filler

tearsheet — a page from a newspaper or magazine that contains an author's printed material

teleplay — a play that is written or adapted for television

trade — books sold primarily through general bookstores (as opposed to texts, academic, or direct mail books) *treatment* — a detailed narrative outline for a proposed teleplay or screenplay

unsolicited manuscript — a manuscript that an editor or publisher receives but did not request

vanity press — publishers who charge authors for the cost to produce the author's work

work-for-hire — work in which an author is commissioned by a publisher to complete a specific assignment; also writing done in the capacity of one's regular employment

74

THE WRITING PROCESS

Writing is a process composed of five major stages. It is a recursive process in which the writer moves back and forth through the various stages. Following are the stages of the writing process along with possible activities in which the writer may engage.

Stages	Possible Activities
I. Prewriting	problem finding
idea generation	questioning
research	role playing
analysis of data	brainstorming
organization	freewriting
topic selection and focus	mapping, clustering
	data gathering
clarification of purpose	interviewing
	writing outlines
	writing leads
	illustrating
II. Writing the draft	writing
	thinking
	rearranging
	alternating between writing and reading
	elaborating
	pausing
	planning

Stages	Possible Activities
III. Revising	polishing
	rethinking
	rearranging
	clarifying
	rewriting
	additional researching
	getting responses
	peer critiquing
	writing conferences
	cutting and pasting
	listening to writing by reading out loud
IV. Editing	proofreading
	final polishing
	correcting of mechanics

V. Publishing
   sharing
   submitting
	readings

	displays
	bulletin boards
	classroom, school publications
	submitting to magazines, newsletters, newspapers